QUICK KNITS

DEBBIE BLISS AND MARY NORDEN

Bell & Hyma

ACKNOWLEDGEMENTS

The authors would like to thank the following for all their help with creating the sweaters for this book: Pat Brooker, Pat Colins, Elaine Craig, Margaret Harmer, Helena Hudsen, Anne Jaggs, Isabel Kemp, Thora Matthews, Joan Morgan, Mrs K Murphy, Hilary Neville, Doreen Sanders, Mary Stenning, Betty Webb and Margaret Yetton.

Published in 1986 by
Bell & Hyman Limited
Denmark House
37/39 Queen Elizabeth Street
London SE1 2QB

© Debbie Bliss and Mary Norden, 1986

British Library Cataloguing in Publication Data

Bliss, Debbie
　　Quick knits.
　　1. Knitting — Patterns
　　I. Title　II. Norden Mary
　　646.4'07　TT820

ISBN 0 7135 2664 5

Designed by Colin Lewis
Photographed by Andy Lane
Make-Up Maggie Baker
Hair Alan Whyte for the Joshua Galvin Salon
Stylist Mariann Leddy
Illustrations Fiona McTague
Typeset by Typecast Photosetting & Printing Ltd.,
East Peckham, Kent.
Printed in Italy

CONTENTS

INTRODUCTION

So often, in fashion simplest is best. With these 20 designs we hope to demonstrate that stylish knits can be created combining basic stitches with easy to wear fashion shapes.

Even though none of the patterns use complicated stitches or techniques, there is still a wide variety of shape, style and texture, and the collection includes garments that are cool or cosy, sporty or sophisticated, casual or classic.

None of the designs are difficult to create — there is a mock cable for those not yet confident enough to use a cable needle; and for the more adventurous, a simple cable to introduce the technique. There are several 2-tone colour sweaters, none of which involve changing colour mid row. These appear to be much more complex than they are.

We have also included a section at the back to illustrate bright ideas to vary the look of the main patterns, giving wider scope to the knitter. People of more experience will be able to think of their own ideas.

We hope you have as much fun knitting these sweaters as we have had designing them.

Debbie Bliss
Mary Norden

STARTING TO KNIT

YARN

To achieve perfect results it is important to use the yarn specified in the pattern. There are tremendous variations in thickness between yarns of the same ply. Buy all your yarn at once, checking that dye lots are identical.

TENSION

The tension is the number of rows and stitches in a given measurement over the knitted fabric. The size of every garment is based on this measurement. Personal tension varies and adjustments in needle size are often necessary. It is therefore absolutely essential before starting to make any garment that you check your tension against the tension of the pattern you are following. This is done by knitting a sample or tension square.

Using the same yarn and stitch indicated in the pattern, work a square measuring at least 10cm (4in) by 10cm (4in). Lay the sample on a flat surface and measure 10cm (4in), or the measurement suggested in the pattern, across stitches and rows. Mark this square with pins. Count the number of stitches and rows in the square. If there are too few, the tension is too loose and a new sample should be worked using smaller needles. If there are too many stitches and rows, a new sample should be worked using larger needles.

CASTING ON WITH TWO NEEDLES

1. Make a slip loop. This is the first stitch to be made. Wrap the yarn twice around two fingers and with the knitting needle pull a loop through the yarn on the fingers. Pull both ends of yarn to tighten the slip loop, and leave on left hand needle.

2. Put the right hand needle through the loop, from front to back, and take the yarn under and over the point of the right hand needle.

3. Draw the yarn through the loop on the left hand needle with the right needle to make another loop or stitch.

4. Place the stitch on the left hand needle.

Repeat steps 2-4 until the required number of stitches have been made.

BASIC STITCHES

Knit stitch and Purl stitch are the two basic knitting stitches.

Knit stitch: abbreviation = K

1. With the needle holding the stitches in your left hand, and the yarn at the back, insert the right hand needle through the front of the first stitch.

2. Take the yarn under and over the point of the right hand needle.

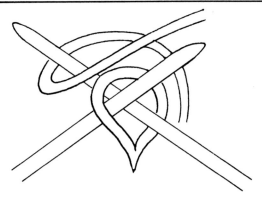

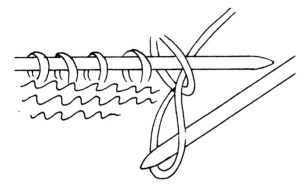

3. Pull the loop through and slide the first stitch off your left hand needle while the new stitch is retained on the right hand needle. Continue in this way until all the stitches are knitted.

The side of work facing you while knitting is known as the knit side.

When every row is knitted, garter stitch is formed and when one row is knitted and the next purled, stocking stitch is formed.

CASTING OFF

1. Knit the first two stitches.

2. Lift the first stitch over the second by inserting the tip of your left hand needle through the first stitch.

3. Drop the first stitch off the needle leaving only the second stitch on the right hand needle.

4. Knit the next stitch.

Repeat steps 2-4 until the required number of stitches have been cast off.

If finishing a piece of work, repeat to the last stitch, cut the yarn and slip the end through the stitch and pull tight.

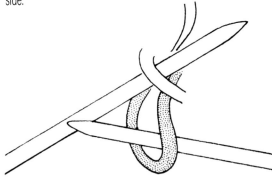

Purl stitch: abbreviation = P

1. With the needle holding the stitches in your left hand and the yarn at the front, insert the right hand needle from the back to the front of the first stitch.

2. Take the yarn over and around the point of the right hand needle.

3. Pull the loop through and slide the first stitch off your left hand needle. Continue in this way until all stitches are purled.

MORE ADVANCED STITCHES

Although these stitches all look more complicated, they are still only variations using K and P.

Double Moss Stitch

(4 st pattern repeat)

1st row (right side): K1, *K2, P2; rep from * to last st, P1.

2nd row: as 1st row.

3rd row: P1, *P2, K2; rep from * to last st, K1.

4th row: as 3rd row.

These 4 rows form patt.

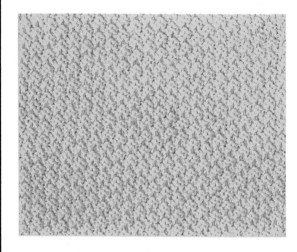

Sand Stitch

(2 st pattern repeat)

1st row (wrong side): K.

2nd row: *K1, P1; rep from * to last st, K1.

These 2 rows form patt.

CABLES

To make cables you will need an additional cable needle. These are small double pointed needles used to hold stitches to be cabled to the front or back of the work when required. Stitches held at the front will twist from right to left when knitted and stitches held at the back will twist from left to right when knitted.

Cable Pattern Panel

This is a typical cable and is worked over 16 sts:

1st row: P2, K12, P2.

2nd and every alternate row: K2, P12, K2.

3rd row: as 1st row.

5th row: P2, sl next 4 sts onto cable needle and leave at back of work, K4, then K4 from cable needle, K4, P2.

7th row: as 1st row.

9th row: as 1st row.

11th row: P2, K4, sl next 4 sts onto cable needle and leave at front of work, K4, then K4 from cable needle, P2.

12th row: as 2nd row.

These 12 rows form patt.

Mock Cables

These cables are very easy to make and look just like the real thing:

1st row (wrong side): K2, P4, K2.
2nd row: P2, K4, P2.
3rd to 5th rows: rep 1st and 2nd rows once and then the 1st row again.
6th row: P2, K into 4th st on left hand needle, then 3rd, then 2nd, then 1st and slip all 4 sts off needle together, P2.
These 6 rows form patt.

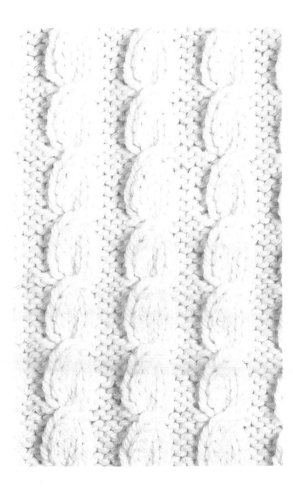

INCREASING

Abbreviation = inc 1 st.
Where blocks of stitches are to be added to a garment to give it shape, casting on is used. To increase a single stitch at any point in a row, increasing is used.

1. In a knit row: knit into the front of the stitch, and without disgarding the stitch on the left hand needle, knit into the back of it, making two stitches.

2. In a purl row: purl into the front of the stitch and without disgarding the stitch on the left hand needle, purl into the back of it, making two stitches.

DECREASING

Abbreviation = either K2 tog or dec 1 st.
When blocks of stitches are to be lost from a garment to give it shape, casting off is used. To loose a single stitch at any point in a row, decreasing is used.

1. In a knit row: decrease one stitch by inserting the right hand needle knit wise into the second and first stitch and then knitting them together as a single stitch.

2. In a purl row: decrease one stitch by inserting the right hand needle purl wise through the first and then the second stitch and then purling them together as a single stitch.

PRESSING

Always press on the wrong side of the garment before making up and only press when necessary. Refer to ball band. Take care not to overpress and avoid pressing any ribbing.

MAKING UP AND DARNING IN THE ENDS

When making up a garment always use the same yarn it was knitted in. Back stitch can be used for most seams. This is worked from the wrong side and the pieces should be pinned

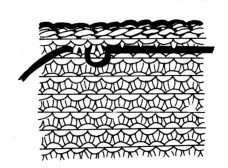

first especially when there is pattern to match. Back stitch provides a simple and firm seam and should be done using a round-pointed wool needle. Join the seam by making small running stitches which overlap.

Flat seaming is used for ribbing. This is also worked from the wrong side and a small running stitch is used. Be careful not to pull too tightly.

For a very neat finish, mattress stitch can be used and should be worked with the right side facing — this does, of course, make matching stripes and patterns much easier.

1. Join the yarn to the fabric. Insert the needle into two bars of the knitting, one stitch in. Take the needle across to the other pieces and pick up the corresponding bars.

2. Repeat down the seam pulling up the yarn every few stitches.

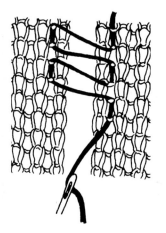 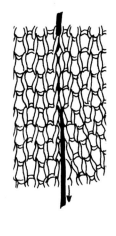

Loose end of yarn should always be darned in both to neaten and secure the fabric. There are two methods of doing this — either darn into the edge of the piece of fabric or oversew along the edge. The end will disappear into the seams of the finished sweater.

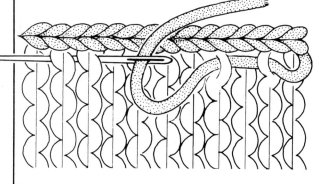

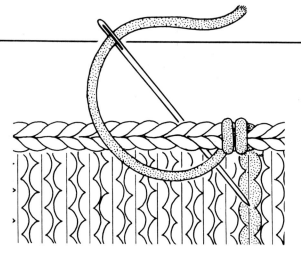

If you should be using blocks of colour in the middle of rows use the ends of yarn to make the joins more secure by overstitching the joins between the two colours.

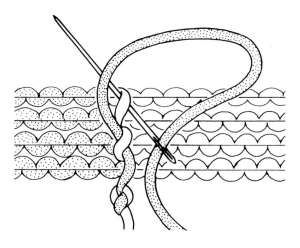

CARE OF KNITTED GARMENTS

It is important to check on the ball band of the yarn used to see if any instructions are given for cleaning.

If hand-washing is indicated, the garment should be washed in warm water, or at the temperature indicated on the ball-band. Use a soap powder that is particularly suitable for knitwear and then rinse thoroughly in tepid water. Squeeze gently to remove excess water and dry flat, patting the garment into shape.

MEASUREMENTS

When there is more than one size to a pattern, the small size is printed first and the larger sizes follow in brackets. This applies throughout the pattern wherever instructions differ according to size. When one instruction is given it applies to all sizes.

NEEDLE SIZES

Metric (in mm)	Britain	USA
9	000	15
8½	00	13
8	0	—
7½	1	11
7	2	10½
6½	3	10
6	4	9
5½	5	8
5	6	7
4½	7	6
4	8	5
3½ and 3¾	9	4
3¼	10	3
2¾ and 3	11	2
2½	12	1
2¼	13	0
2	14	00

ABBREVIATIONS

alts	alternate
beg	beginning
cm	centimetre(s)
cont	continue
dec	decrease
foll	following
in	inch(es)
inc	increase
K	knit
K1 b	K 1 below, insert the right needle through the centre of the stitch below the next stitch to be knitted so that both stitches are knitted at the same time
P	purl
patt	pattern
psso	pass slipped st over
rem	remain
rep	repeat
sl	slip
st(s)	stitch(es)
st-st	stocking stitch, K on right side and P back
TBL	through back of loop
tog	together

SPINNERS & SUPPLIERS

HAYFIELD
Hayfield Textiles Limited, Hayfield Mills, Glusburn, Nr. Keighley, W. Yorkshire BD20 8QP

EMU
Emu Wools Limited, Leeds Road, Greengates, Bradford, W. Yorkshire BD10 9TE

ROWAN
Rowan, Green Lane Mill, Washpit, Holmfirth, W. Yorkshire HD7 1RW

FRENCH WOOLS LIMITED (Pingouin)
7-11 Lexington Street, London W1R 4BU

SCHEEPJESWOL UK LTD
7 Colemeadow Road, Redditch, Worcestershire

WENDY WOOLS
Carter and Parker Ltd, Gordon Mills, Netherfield Road, Guiseley, Leeds LS20 9PD

W.H. SMITH WOOLSHOPS
Strand House, Greenbridge Industrial Estate, Greenbridge Road, Swindon SN3 3LD

PHILDAR YARNS
Phildar (UK) Ltd, 4 Gambrel Road, Westgate Industrial Estate, Northampton NN5 5NF

SUNBEAM WOOLS
Crawshaw Mills, Pudsey, West Yorkshire LS28 7BS

RIES WOOLS OF HOLBORN
242-3 High Holborn, London WC1V 7DZ

WELL SUITED

WELL SUITED

A tunic and skirt with matching mock cables — so simple and no need to use a cabling needle!

TUNIC

MATERIALS

18 (19, 20) 50g balls Hayfield Grampian Chunky. Pair each 5½mm and 6½mm knitting needles. 3 buttons.

MEASUREMENTS

To fit 86 (91, 96)cm (34 (36, 38)in) bust; length from shoulder 76 (78, 80)cm (30 (30¾, 31½)in); sleeve seam 45 (45, 46)cm (17½ (17½, 18)in). Figures in brackets refer to larger sizes.

TENSION

18 sts and 19 rows to 10cm (4in) over patt on 6½mm needles.

BACK

Using 5½mm needles cast on 98 (106, 114) sts and work 8cm (3¼in)in K1, P1 rib. Change to 6½mm needles and work in patt as follows.

1st row (wrong side): K3, *P4, K4; rep from * to end, ending last rep K3.
2nd row: P3, *K4, P4; rep from * to end, ending last rep P3.
3rd to 5th rows: rep 1st and 2nd rows once and then the 1st row again.
6th row: P3, *K into 4th st on left hand needle, then 3rd, then 2nd, then 1st and slip all 4 sts off needle together, P4; rep from * to end, ending last rep P3.
These 6 rows form the patt. Rep these 6 rows until work measures 49 (50, 51)cm (19¼ (19½, 20)in) from cast-on edge. Mark each end of row with contrast thread. Continue in patt until work measures 76 (78, 80)cm (30 (30¾, 31½)in) from cast-on edge, ending with a wrong side row.

Shape Shoulders: cast off 17 (18, 20) sts at beg of next 2 rows, 17 (19, 20) sts at beg of foll 2 rows. Leave rem 30 (32, 34) sts on a holder.

FRONT

Work as given for back until work measures 58 (60, 62)cm (23 (23¾, 24½)in) from cast-on edge, ending with a wrong side row.

Front Opening: patt 45 (49, 53) sts, leave rem sts on spare needle, turn and patt back. Cont straight until work measures 66 (68, 70)cm (26 (26¾, 27½)in) from cast-on edge, ending with a right side row.

Shape Neck: cont in patt cast off 3 (3, 4) sts at beg of next row, patt one row, cast off 2 sts at beg of foll row. Dec one st at neck edge on next and every foll row until 34 (37, 40) sts rem. Cont straight until work measures same as back to shoulder, ending at side edge.

Shape Shoulder: cont in patt cast off 17 (18, 20) sts at beg of next row, patt one row. Cast off rem 17 (19, 20) sts. Return to sts on spare needle. Rejoin yarn and cast off centre 8 sts. Cont to match first side reversing shapings.

SLEEVES

Using 5½mm needles cast on 50 (52, 54) sts and work 8cm (3¼in) in K1, P1 rib, inc 8 (10, 12) sts evenly across last row. 58 (62, 66) sts. Change to 6½mm needles. Next row: K3 (5, 3), * P4, K4; rep from * to end, ending last rep K3 (5, 3). This row sets the position of patt, cont in patt as on back, inc one st at each end of next alternate row, then on every foll 3rd row until there are 98 (100, 104) sts. Cont straight in patt until sleeve seam measures 45 (45, 46)cm (17½ (17½, 18)in) from cast-on edge. Cast off.

NECKBAND

Using 5½mm needles, pick up and K15 sts up right front neck, K30 (32, 34) sts across back neck from holder, pick up and K15 sts down left front neck. 60 (62, 64) sts. Work 6 rows in K1, P1 rib. Cast off in rib.

BUTTON BAND

Using 5½mm needles and with right side facing, pick up and K 26 sts down neckband and left side edge. Work 10 rows in K1, P1 rib. Cast off in rib.

BUTTONHOLE BAND

Using 5½mm needles and with right side facing, pick up and K 26 sts up right side edge and neckband. Work 4 rows in K1, P1 rib. Buttonhole row: rib 4, * cast off 2, rib 6; rep from * to end, ending last rep rib 4. Next row: rib to end, casting on 2 over those cast off. Rib 4 rows straight. Cast off.

TO MAKE UP

Sew in sleeves between markers, placing centre of sleeves to shoulder seams. Join side and sleeve seams. Lap right front band over left and sew lower ends to the cast off sts at centre front. Sew on buttons.

SKIRT

MATERIALS

6 (7, 7) 50g balls Hayfield Grampian DK. Pair each 3¼mm and 4mm knitting needles. 2.5cm (1in) wide elastic to fit waist.

MEASUREMENTS

To fit 81 (86, 92)cm (32 (34, 36)in) hips; length 58 (60, 62)cm (23 (23¾, 24½)in). Figures in brackets refer to larger sizes.

TENSION

30 sts and 32 rows to 10cm (4in) over patt on 4mm needles.

BACK AND FRONT ALIKE

Using 3¼mm needles cast on 130 (138, 146) sts and work 3cm (1¼in) in K1, Pi rib. Change to 4mm needles, work in patt as follows.

1st row (wrong side): K3, *P4, K4; rep from * to end, ending last row K3.

2nd row: P3, *K4, P4; rep from * to end, ending last rep P3.

3rd to 5th rows: rep 1st and 2nd rows once and then the 1st row again.

6th row: P3, *K into 4th st on left hand needle, then 3rd, then 2nd, then 1st and slip all 4 sts off needle together, P4; rep from * to end, ending last rep P3.

These 6 rows form the patt. Rep these 6 rows until work measures 54 (56, 58)cm (21¼ (22, 23¾)in) from cast-on edge, ending with a wrong side row. Change to 3¼mm needles and work 8cm (3¼in) in K1, P1 rib. Cast off in rib.

TO MAKE UP

Join side seams. Fold rib over at waist in half to wrong side and slip stitch in place, leaving an opening to thread elastic. Thread elastic and sew ends together to fit waist. Close opening.

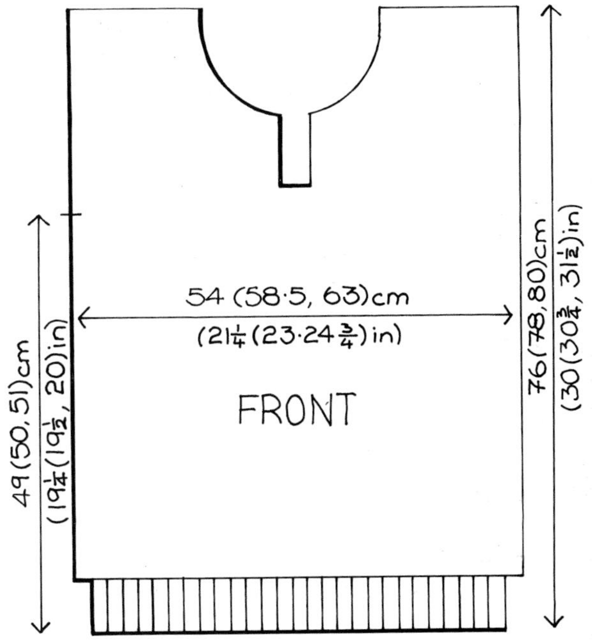
54 (58·5, 63)cm
(21¼ (23·24¾) in)
FRONT
49 (50, 51)cm
(19¼ (19½, 20) in)
76 (78, 80)cm
(30 (30¾, 31½) in)

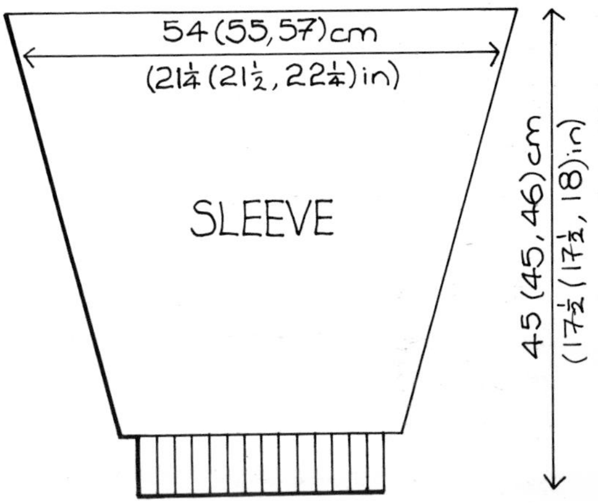
54 (55, 57)cm
(21¼ (21½, 22¼) in)
SLEEVE
45 (45, 46)cm
(17½ (17½, 18) in)

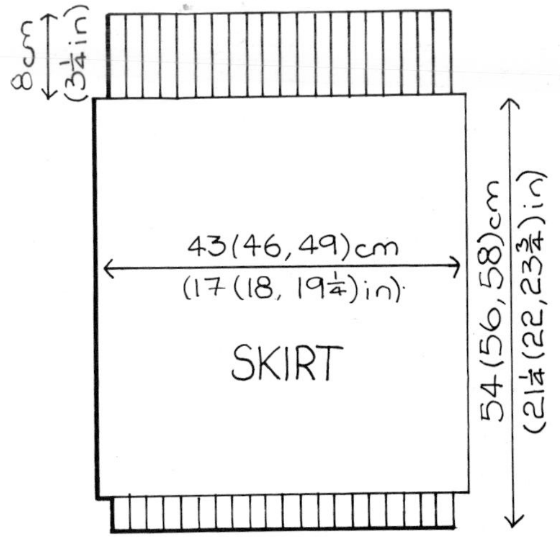
8cm
(3¼ in)
43 (46, 49)cm
(17 (18, 19¼) in)
SKIRT
54 (56, 58)cm
(21¼ (22, 23¾) in)

MIXED DOUBLES

This warm, winter sweater with cosy shawl collar has a tweedy effect created by knitting the two colours simultaneously.

MATERIALS

8 (9, 10) 50g balls of Hayfield Grampian DK in main colour **(A)**; 7 (7, 8) 50g balls in contrast colour **(B)**; Pair each 5½mm and 6½mm knitting needles.

MEASUREMENTS

To fit 86 (91, 96)cm (34 (36, 38)in) bust; length from shoulder 68 (70, 72)cm (26¾ (27½, 28¼)in); sleeve seam 46cm (18in) for all sizes. Figures in brackets refer to larger sizes.

TENSION

15 sts and 21 rows to 10cm (4in) over st-st on 6½mm needles.

NOTE

Main and contrast colours are used together throughout, except for collar where main is used double.

BACK

Using 5½mm needles and with A and B together, cast on 68 (72, 76) sts and work 8cm (3¼in) in K1, P1 rib, increasing 20 sts evenly across last row. 88 (92, 96) sts. Change to 6½mm needles and work in st-st until work measures 40 (41, 42)cm (15¾ (16, 16½)in) from cast-on edge, ending with a P row. Mark each end of row with a contrast thread. Cont in st-st until work measures 68 (70, 72)cm (26¾ (27½, 28¼)in) from cast-on edge, ending with a P row.

Shape Shoulders: Cast off 30 (31, 32) sts at beg of next 2 rows. Cast off rem 28 (30, 32) sts.

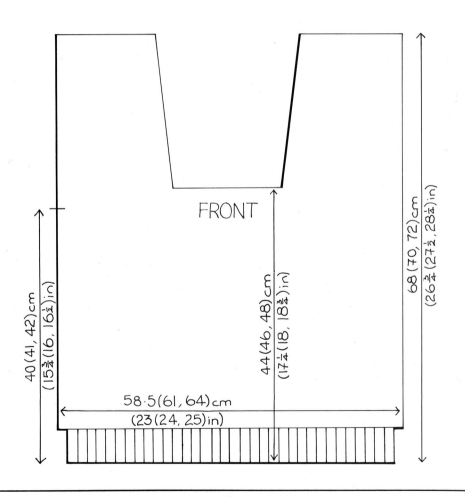

FRONT

40 (41, 42)cm (15¾ (16, 16½)in)

44 (46, 48)cm (17¼ (18, 18¾)in)

68 (70, 72)cm (26¾ (27½, 28¼)in)

58·5 (61, 64)cm (23 (24, 25)in)

FRONT

Work as given for back until work measures 44 (46, 48)cm (17¼ (18, 18¾)in) from cast-on edge, ending with a P row.

Shape Neck: K 34 (35, 36) sts, cast off next 20 (22, 24) sts, K to end. Cont on last set of sts only for first side. Dec one st at neck edge on next row, then following 4th row and then on every 8th row until 30 (31, 32) sts remain. Cont straight until work measures same as back to shoulder, ending with a P row. Cast off.

Return to rem 30 (31, 32) sts, with wrong-side facing, rejoin yarns and P to end. Cont to match first side reversing shapings.

SLEEVES

Using 5½mm needles and with A and B together, cast on 40 (42, 42) sts and work 8cm (3¼in) in K1, P1 rib, increasing 12 (12, 14) sts evenly across last row. 52 (54, 56) sts. Change to 6½mm needles and work in st-st, increasing one st at each end of next and every foll 4th row until there are 86 (90, 94) sts. Cont straight until sleeve seam measures 46cm (18in) from cast-on edge, ending with a P row. Cast off.

COLLAR

First join shoulder seams. Using 5½mm needles and A double, cast on 118 (120, 122) sts and work 13 (14, 15)cm (5 (5½, 6)in) in K1, P1 rib. Cast off in rib.

TO MAKE UP

Press work according to instructions on ball band. Sew cast-off edge of sleeve to body between markers. Join side and sleeve seams. Sew cast-on edge of collar to neck edge, beg at right front shaping. Cross right half of collar over left at centre front and sew row ends of collar to cast-off sts on body.

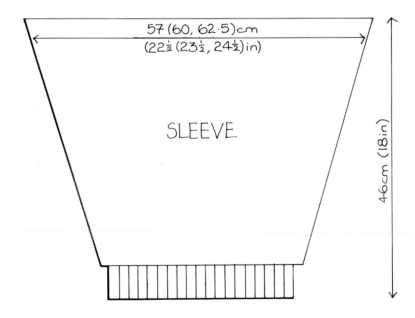

57 (60, 62·5)cm
(22½ (23½, 24½)in)

SLEEVE

46cm (18in)

NIFTY

NAUTICAL

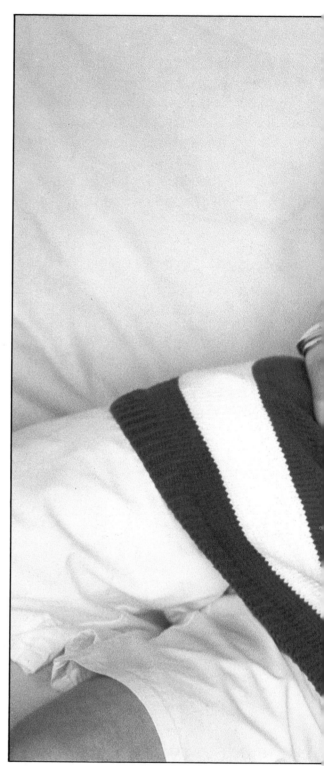

NIFTY NAUTICAL

Easy-knit stripes for the stylish mariner.

MATERIALS

8 (9, 9) 50g balls Phildar Detente in navy **(N)**; 7 (7, 8) balls in white **(W)**. Pair each 2¼mm and 3mm knitting needles.

MEASUREMENTS

To fit 86 (91, 96)cm (34 (36, 38)in) bust; length from shoulder 66cm (26in); sleeve seam 42cm (16¼in) for all sizes. Figures in brackets refer to larger sizes.

TENSION

22 sts and 33 rows to 10cm (4in) over st-st on 3mm needles.

BACK AND FRONT ALIKE

Using 2¼mm needles and N cast on 116 (122, 128) sts and work 3cm (1¼in) in K1, P1 rib. Change to 3mm needles and work 10 rows in st-st. * Change to W and work 20 rows in st-st. Change to N and work 20 rows in st-st. Repeat from *

3 times more and at the same time place a marker at each end of row when work measures 42 (41, 40)cm (16½ (16¼, 16)in) from cast-on edge, ending with a P row. Work a further 20 rows in W and then 10 rows in N. Still using 3mm needles and N work 3cm (1¼in) in K1, P1 rib. Cast off in rib.

SLEEVES

Using 2¼mm needles and N cast on 62 (66, 70) sts and work 3cm (1¼in) in K1, P1 rib. Change to 3mm needles and work in stripe pattern as on back/front, inc one st at each end of next and every foll 4th row until there are 122 (126, 130) sts. Cont straight in stripe patt until 40 row patt has been repeated 3 times in all. Cast off.

TO MAKE UP

Lap back top rib over front at shoulders for 6cm (2¼in) from outer edge. Sew in sleeves, placing centre of sleeves to shoulder seams and cast-off edge of sleeves to body between markers. Join side and sleeve seams.

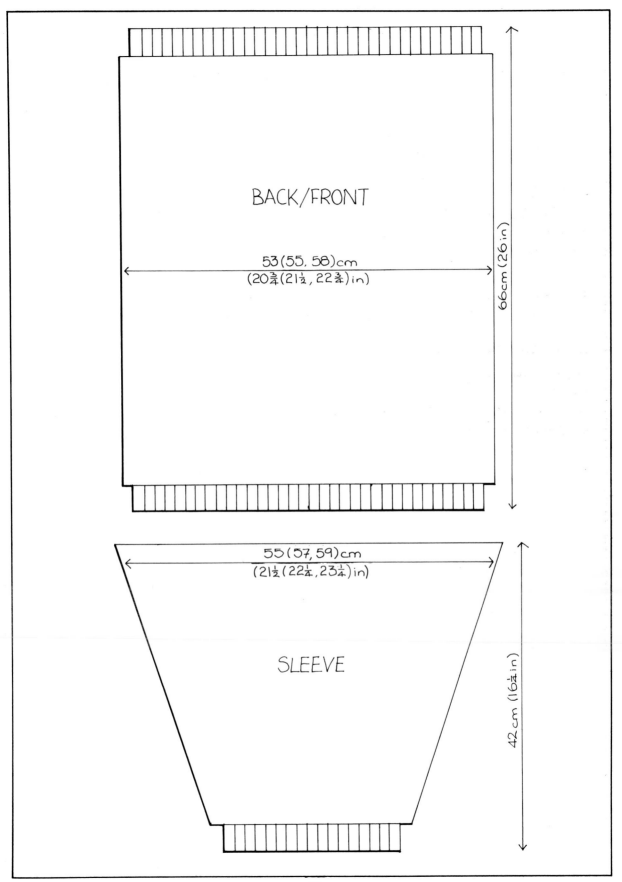

BACK/FRONT

53(55, 58)cm
(20¾(21½, 22¾)in)

66cm(26in)

55(57, 59)cm
(21½(22¼, 23¼)in)

SLEEVE

42cm(16½in)

IN THE PINK

IN THE PINK

A versatile cardigan in a textured mohair. Deliciously soft and simple to make.

MATERIALS

9 (9, 10) 50g balls Hayfield Lugano Fancy. Pair each 5mm and 6mm knitting needles. 5 buttons.

MEASUREMENTS

To fit 86 (91, 96)cm (34 (36, 38)in) bust; length from shoulder 61 (63, 65)cm (24 (24¾, 25¾)in); sleeve seam 46cm (18in) for all sizes. Figures in brackets refer to larger sizes.

TENSION

16 sts and 20 rows to 10cm (4in) over st-st on 6mm needles.

BACK

Using 5mm needles cast on 71 (77, 83) sts.
1st row: *K1, P1; rep from * to last st, K1.
2nd row: *P1, K1; rep from * to last st, P1.
Repeat these 2 rows for 12cm (5in), increasing 25 sts evenly across last row. 96 (102, 108) sts. Change to 6mm needles and work in st-st until work measures 36 (37, 38)cm (14¼ (14¾, 15)in) from cast-on edge, ending with a P row.

Shape Armholes: cast off 10 (11, 12) sts at beg of next 2 rows. 76 (80, 84) sts. Cont straight until armholes measure 25 (26, 27)cm (10 (10½, 11)in), ending with a P row.

Shape Shoulders: cast off 12 (12, 13) sts at beg of next 2 rows, 12 (13, 13) sts at beg of foll 2 rows. Cast off rem 28 (30, 32) sts.

RIGHT FRONT

Using 5mm needles cast on 41 (43, 45) sts and work 2cm (¾in) in rib as on back, ending with a 2nd rib row.
1st buttonhole row: rib 3, cast off 4 sts, rib to end.
2nd buttonhole row: rib to end casting on 4 sts over those cast off.

Cont in rib as on back, working 2 more buttonholes when work measures 7cm (2¾in) and 11cm (4½in). Work one row, thus ending with a 1st rib row.
Next row: rib 1 (2, 1), *inc in next st, K1; repeat from * to last 10 (11, 10) sts, rib 0 (1, 0), place next 10 sts on a safety pin. 46 (48, 52) sts. Change to 6mm needles and work in st-st until work measures 26cm (10in) from cast-on edge, ending at neck edge.

Shape Front Edge: dec one st at beg of next and every foll 5th row, 5 times in all and then on every foll 6th row until 24 (25, 26) sts rem, AT THE SAME TIME, when work measures same as back to armhole, cast off 10 (11, 12) sts at armhole edge. Cont straight until work measures same as back to shoulders, ending at side edge.

Shape Shoulder: cast off 12 (12, 13) sts at beg of next row. Work one row. Cast off rem 12 (13, 13) sts.

LEFT FRONT

Work to match right front, reversing all shaping and omitting buttonholes.

SLEEVES

Using 5mm needles cast on 37 (39, 41) sts and work 10cm (4in) in rib as on back, increasing 7 (9, 11) sts evenly across last row. 44 (48, 52) sts. Change to 6mm needles and work in st-st, increasing one st at each end of next and every foll 3rd row until there are 88 (92, 96) sts. Cont straight until sleeve seam measures 46cm (18in). Mark each end of row with a coloured thread. Work a further 6 (7, 7.5)cm (2½ (2¾, 3)in). Cast off. Join shoulder seams.

BUTTONBAND

Using 5mm needles and with right side facing rib 10 sts from safety pin on left front, increasing one st in first st. 11 sts. Work in rib until band, when slightly stretched, fits up front edge to centre back neck. Cast off in rib. Tack band in place and mark position of 2 more buttons, 1st at beg of front shaping and 2nd spaced equally between last one worked and one on welt.

BUTTONHOLE BAND

Using 5mm needles and with wrong side facing rib 10 sts from safety pin on right front, increasing one st in first st. 11 sts. Complete to match buttonband, working buttonholes where indicated on buttonband.

TO MAKE UP

Sew bands to front. Sew tops of sleeves from markers to cast-off sts on body. Sew in sleeves. Join side and sleeve seams. Sew on buttons.

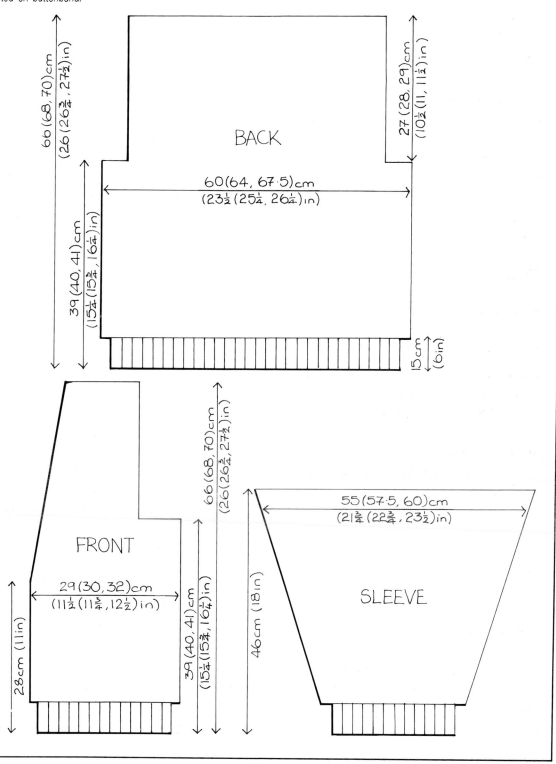

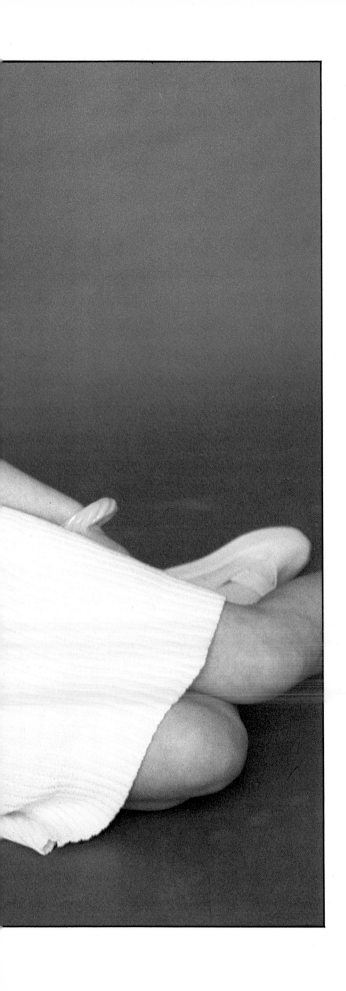

L
E
M
O
N

D
R
O
P

LEMON DROP

Wide and short in double moss stitch — still only knitting and purling.

MATERIALS

10 (10, 11) 50g balls Emu Superwash DK. Pair each 3¼mm and 4mm knitting needles.

MEASUREMENTS

To fit 86 (91, 96)cm (34 (36, 38)in) bust; length from shoulder 39 (41, 43)cm (15¼ (16, 17½)in); sleeve seam 35cm (13¾in) for all sizes. Figures in brackets refer to larger sizes.

TENSION

23 sts and 36 rows to 10cm (4in) over patt on 4mm needles.

BACK

Using 3¼mm needles cast on 122 (130, 138) sts and work 6cm (2¼in) in K1, P1 rib. Change to 4mm needles and work in patt as follows.
1st row (right side): K1, *K2, P2; rep from * to last st, P1.
2nd row: as 1st row.
3rd row: P1, *P2, K2; rep from * to last st, K1.
4th row: as 3rd row.
These 4 rows form patt. Cont in pattern until work measures 13 (14, 15)cm (5 (5½, 6)in) from cast-on edge, ending with a wrong side row.

Shape Armholes: Cast off 13 (14, 15) sts at beg of next 2 rows. 96 (102, 108) sts. Cont in patt until work measures 30 (32, 34)cm (11¾ (12½, 13¼)in) from cast-on edge, ending with a wrong side row.

Shape Neck: Patt 30 (32, 34) sts, turn and leave rem sts on a spare needle. Patt one row. Dec one st at neck edge on next and every foll 3rd row until 22 (24, 26) sts rem. Cont straight until work measures 39 (41, 43)cm (15¼ (16, 17½)in) from cast-on edge, ending at side edge.

Shape Shoulders: Cast off 22 (24, 26) sts. Return to sts on spare needle. With right side facing slip centre 36 (38, 40) sts onto a holder, rejoin yarn and complete to match first side reversing shapings.

FRONT

Work as for back but place pocket as follows. After 23 (24, 25)cm (9 (9½, 10)in) have been worked, from cast-on edge, and with right side facing, patt 12 (15, 18) sts, place next 22 sts onto a holder, cast on 22 sts onto left hand needle and patt to end. Complete as for back.

SLEEVES

Using 3¼mm needles cast on 64 (72, 80) sts and work 6cm (2¼in) in K1, P1 rib. Change to 4mm needles and work in patt, as given on back, inc one st at each end of next and every foll 3rd row until there are 128 (134, 140) sts. Cont straight until sleeve seam measures 35cm (13¾in) from cast-on edge. Mark each end of row with a contrast thread. Work a further 20 (22, 24) rows. Cast off.

NECKBAND

Join right shoulder seam. Using 3¼mm needles pick up and K 28 sts down left front neck, K 36 (38, 40) sts across centre front, pick up and K 28 sts up right front neck, 28 sts down right back neck, K 36 (38, 40) sts across centre back and finally pick up and K 28 sts up left back neck. 184 (188, 192) sts. Work 3cm (1¼in) in K1, P1 rib. Cast off in rib.

POCKET TOP

Return to sts on holder at front, using 4mm needles work 2cm (¾in) in K1, P1 rib. Cast off in rib.

POCKET LINING

With right side facing, using 4mm needles in right hand, pick up 22 sts previously cast-on and work 7 cm (2¾in) in st-st. Cast off.

TO MAKE UP

Join left shoulder and neckband seam. Sew top of sleeves from markers to cast-off sts on body. Sew in sleeves, placing centre to shoulder seams. Join side and sleeve seams. Sew pocket lining in place and carefully sew sides of pocket top to front.

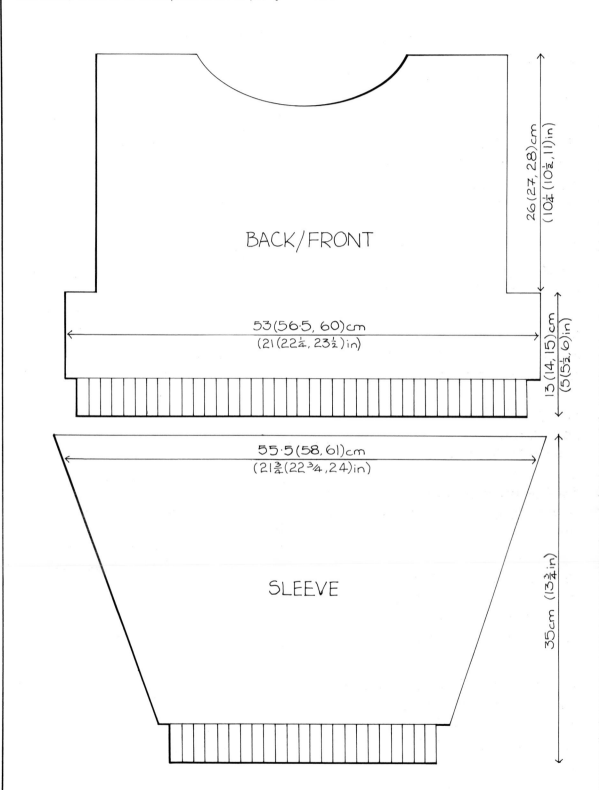

BACK/FRONT

53(56·5, 60)cm
(21(22¼, 23½)in)

26(27, 28)cm
(10¼(10½, 11)in)

13(14, 15)cm
(5(5½, 6)in)

55·5(58, 61)cm
(21¾(22¾, 24)in)

SLEEVE

35cm (13¾in)

Hoodwinked

HOODWINKED

Decidedly dull days need bright, vivid colours. Use quick to knit mohair for this soft, snug jumper with large polo neck.

MATERIALS

11(12, 13) 50g balls Hayfield Lugano Plan. Pair each 5mm and 5½mm knitting needles.

MEASUREMENTS

To fit 81-86 (91-96, 102-107)cm (32-34 (36-38, 40-42)in) bust; length from shoulder 47.5 (50, 52.5)cm (18½ (19¾, 20½)in); sleeve seam 34 (36.5, 37.5)cm (13¼ (14¼, 14¾)in). Figures in brackets refer to larger sizes.

TENSION

14 sts and 28 rows to 10cm (4in) over patt on 5½mm needles.

BACK

Using 5mm needles cast on 75 (79, 83) sts.
1st row: *K1, P1; rep from * to last st, K1.
2nd row: *P1, K1; rep from * to last st, P1.
Rep these 2 rows once more.
Change to 5½mm needles and work in patt as follows.
1st row: K to end.
2nd row: *K1, K1b; rep from * to last st, K1.
Rep these 2 rows until work measures 47.5 (50, 52.5)cm (18½ (19¾, 20½)in) from cast-on edge, ending with a 2nd row. Cast off loosely.

FRONT

Work as given for back until work measures 27.5 (29, 30.5)cm (11 (11½, 12)in) from cast-on edge, ending with a 2nd row.

Divide for V Neck: K36 (38, 40), K2 tog, turn and leave rem sts on a spare needle. Patt one row. Dec one st at neck edge on next row and every foll 4th row until 24 (25, 27) sts rem. Patt 3 rows straight. Cast off. With right side of work facing, rejoin yarn to sts on spare needle and K to end. Continue to match first side reversing shaping.

SLEEVES

Using 5mm needles cast on 47 (49, 51) sts and work 4 rows in rib as on back. Change to 5½mm needles. Work 6 rows straight in patt. Inc one st at each end of next row and every foll 6th row until there are 75 (79, 83) sts. Patt 6 (8, 4) rows straight. Cast off.

POLO NECK

Join right shoulder seam. With right side facing, using 5mm needles pick up and K 56 (58, 62) sts down left front neck edge, pick up loop between sts at centre front and K into back of it and mark it with a contrast thread, then pick up and K 56 (58, 62) sts up right front edge, finally pick up and K 27 (29, 29) sts across centre back. 140 (146, 154) sts.
1st row: *K1, P1; rep from * to within 2 sts of marked st, P2 tog, P marked st, P2 tog TBL, rib to end.
2nd row: rib to within 2 sts of marked st, sl 1 K1, psso, K marked st, K2 tog, rib to end.
Rep these 2 rows for 9cm (3½in). Now continue without decreasing at centre front until work measures 32cm (12½in) (or length required). Cast off in rib.

TO MAKE UP

Join remaining shoulder seam, carrying seam across neckband. Sew in sleeves, placing centre of sleeves to shoulder seams. Join side and sleeve seams.

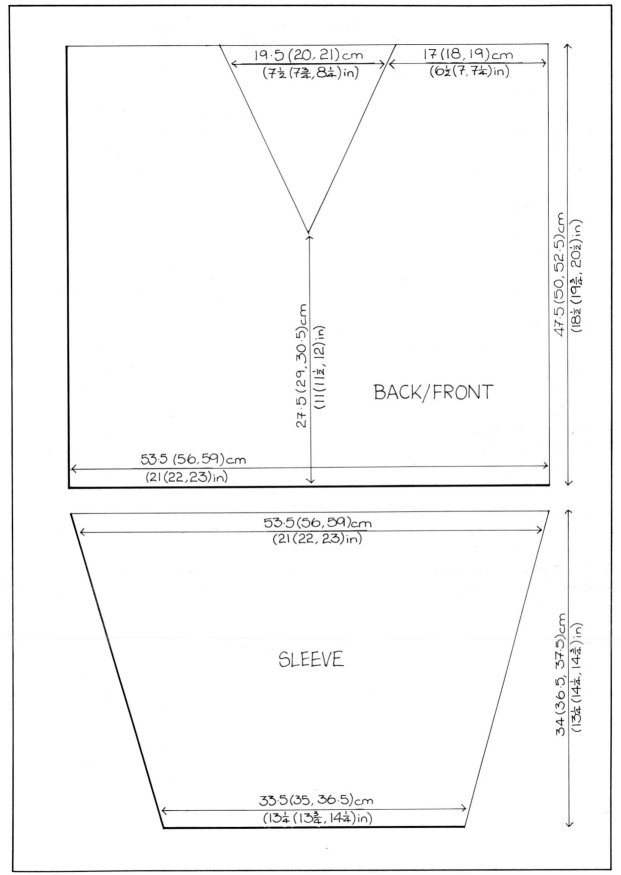

19.5 (20, 21) cm
(7½ (7¾, 8¼) in)

17 (18, 19) cm
(6½ (7, 7¼) in)

47.5 (50, 52.5) cm
(18½ (19¾, 20½) in)

27.5 (29, 30.5) cm
(11 (11½, 12) in)

BACK/FRONT

53.5 (56, 59) cm
(21 (22, 23) in)

53.5 (56, 59) cm
(21 (22, 23) in)

SLEEVE

34 (36.5, 37.5) cm
(13¼ (14¼, 14¾) in)

33.5 (35, 36.5) cm
(13¼ (13¾, 14¼) in)

COUNTRY STYLE

COUNTRY STYLE

The only decoration on this simple sweater is the centre cable. It is a straightforward introduction to a technique seen in more ornate forms on aran knits.

MATERIALS

15 (16, 17) 50g balls Sunbeam Aran Tweed. Pair each 4mm and 5mm knitting needles. Cable needle.

MEASUREMENTS

To fit 86 (91, 96)cm (34 (36, 38)in) bust; length from shoulder 56 (58, 60)cm (22 (22¾, 23½)in); sleeve seam 46cm (18in) for all sizes. Figures in brackets refer to larger sizes.

TENSION

18 sts and 24 rows to 10cm (4in) over st-st on 5mm needles.

CABLE PATTERN PANEL (worked over 16 sts)

1st row: P2, K12, P2.

2nd and every alternate row: K2, P12, K2.

3rd row: as 1st row.

5th row: P2, sl next 4 sts onto cable needle and leave at back of work, K4, then K4 from cable needle, K4, P2.

7th row: as 1st row.

9th row: as 1st row.

11th row: P2, K4, sl next 4 sts onto cable needle and leave at front of work, K4, then K4 from cable needle, P2.

12th row: as 2nd row.

These 12 rows set the centre front cable panel.

BACK

Using 4mm needles cast on 76 (80, 84) sts and work 8cm (3¼in) in K1, P1 rib, inc 20 sts evenly across last row. 96 (100, 104) sts. Change to 5mm needles and work in st-st until work measures 33 (34, 35)cm (13 (13½, 14)in) from cast-on edge, ending with a P row.

Shape Armholes: cast off 9 sts at beg of next 2 rows. 78 (82, 86) sts. Cont in st-st until work measures 56 (58, 60)cm (22 (22¾, 23½)in) from cast-on edge, ending with a P row.

Shape Shoulders: cast off 11 (12, 12) sts at beg of next 2 rows, 12 (12, 13) sts at beg of foll 2 rows. Leave rem 32 (34, 36) sts on a holder.

FRONT

Using 4mm needles cast on 76 (80, 84) sts and work 8cm (3¼in) in K1, P1 rib, inc 24 sts evenly across last row. 100 (104, 108) sts. Change to 5mm needles and work as follows.

Next row: K42 (44, 46), work 1st row of cable patt over next 16 sts, K to end.

Next row: P42 (44, 46), work 2nd row of cable patt over next 16 sts, P to end.

These 2 rows set the position of cable patt. Cont in st-st and cable patt until work measures same as back to armholes, ending with a wrong-side row.

Shape Armholes: cast off 9 sts at beg of next 2 rows. 82 (86, 90) sts. Cont in st-st until work measures 47 (49, 51)cm (18½ (19¼, 20)in) from cast-on edge, ending with a wrong-side row.

Shape Neck: K31 (32, 33) sts, leave rem sts on spare needle. Dec one st at neck edge on next and every foll alternate row until 23 (24, 25) sts rem. Cont straight until work measures same as back to shoulder, ending at armhole edge.

Shape Shoulders: cast off 11 (12, 12) sts at beg of next row. Work one row. Cast off 12 (12, 13) sts. Return to sts on spare needle, slip first 20 (22, 24) sts onto a holder, rejoin yarn to rem 31 (32, 33) sts and K to end. Complete to match first side reversing shaping.

SLEEVES

Using 4mm needles cast on 40 (42, 42) sts and work 8cm (3¼in) in K1, P1 rib, inc 10 (10, 12) sts evenly across last row. 50 (52, 54) sts. Change to 5mm needles and work in st-st inc one st at each end of next and every foll alternate row until there are 90 (94, 98) sts. Cont straight until work measures 46cm (18in) from cast-on edge, ending with a P row. Mark each end of last row with a contrast thead. Work a further 5cm (2in) in st-st. Cast off. Join right shoulder seam.

NECKBAND

Using 4mm needles pick up and K 18 sts down left front neck edge, K 20 (22, 24) sts across centre front, pick up and K 18 sts up right front neck edge, K 32 (34, 36) sts across back neck edge. 88 (92, 96) sts. Work 9cm (3½in) in K1, P1 rib. Cast off in rib.

TO MAKE UP

Join remaining shoulder seam. Sew top of sleeves from markers to cast-off sts on body. Sew in sleeves, placing centre of sleeves to shoulder seams. Join side and sleeve seams.

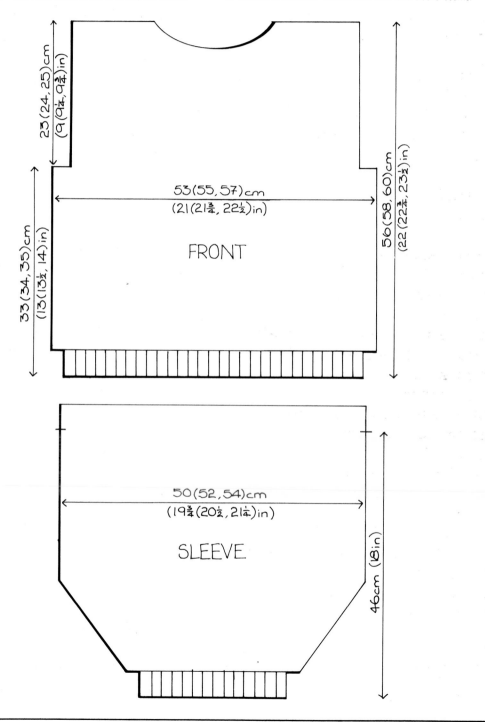

RED HOT!

RED HOT!

Ever needed a splash of colour to add warmth? This oversized, cabled slipover will do just that.

MATERIALS

16 (18) 50g balls Phildar Kadischa. Pair each 5mm and 6mm knitting needles. Cable needle.

MEASUREMENTS

To fit 86-91 (96-102)cm (34-36 (38-40)in) bust loosely; length to shoulder 68 (71)cm (26¾ (28)in) for both sizes. Figures in brackets refer to larger size.

TENSION

15 sts and 22 rows to 10cm (4in) over patt on 6mm needles.

BACK

Using 5mm needles cast on 80 (88) sts and work 6cm (2½in) in K1, P1 rib, inc 4 sts evenly across last row. 84 (92) sts. Change to 6mm needles and work in patt as follows.
1st row (right side): P1, K1, P1, (K1, P1, K1, P1) 0 (1) times, * (K1, P1) 4 times, K1, P2, K10, P2; rep from * to last 12 (16) sts, K1, P1 to end.
2nd row: P1, K1, P1, (K1, P1, K1, P1) 0 (1) times, * (K1, P1) 4 times, K3, P10, K2; rep from * to last 12 (16) sts, K1, P1 to end.
3rd to 6th rows: rep 1st and 2nd rows twice more.
7th row: P1, K1, P1, (K1, P1, K1, P1) 0 (1) times, * (K1, P1) 4 times, K1, P2, slip next 5 sts onto cable needle and hold at back of work, K next 5 sts then K5 from cable needle, P2; rep from * to last 12 (16) sts, K1, P1 to end.
8th row: as 2nd row.
9th to 12th rows: rep 1st and 2nd rows twice more.
These 12 rows form patt and are rep throughout. Cont in patt until work measures 43 (45)cm (17 (17¾)in) from cast-on edge, ending with a wrong side row.

Shape Armholes: cast off 4 (5) sts at beg of next 2 rows. Cont straight in patt until work measures 68 (71)cm (26¾ (28)in) from cast-on edge, ending with a wrong side row.

Shape Shoulders: cast off 22 (24) sts at beg of next 2 rows. Leave rem 32 (34) sts on a holder.

FRONT

Work as given for back until work measures 33 (36)cm (13 (14¼)in) from cast-on edge, ending with a wrong side row.

Shape V Neck: patt 42 (46) sts, turn and leave rem sts on a spare needle. Patt one row. Dec one st at neck edge on next row and every foll 4th row until 32 (36) sts rem, then on every foll 6th row until 22 (24) sts rem, AT THE SAME TIME, work armholes as on back. Cont straight until work measures same as back to shoulder, ending at armhole edge.

Shape Shoulder: cast off 22 (24) sts. Return to sts on spare needle and with right side of work facing slip centre st onto a safety pin, rejoin yarn to rem 41 (45) sts and patt to end. Complete to match first side, reversing shapings.

NECKBAND

Join right shoulder seam. Using 5mm needles and with right side facing pick up and K 80 sts down left front neck edge, K front neck st and mark it with a coloured thread, pick up and K 80 sts up right front neck edge and finally K 32 (34) across back neck edge. 193 (195) sts.
1st row: *K1, P1; rep from * to within 2 sts of marked st, K2 tog, P1, K2 tog TBL, rib to end.
2nd row: rib to within 2 sts of marked st, P2 tog TBL, K1, P2 tog, rib to end.
Rep these 2 rows twice more and then the 1st row again. Cast off in rib, still dec at centre front.

ARMBANDS

Join left shoulder seam. Using 5mm needles pick up and K 96 (98) sts around armholes. Work 3cm (1¼in) in K1, P1 rib. Cast off in rib.

TO MAKE UP

Join side seams.

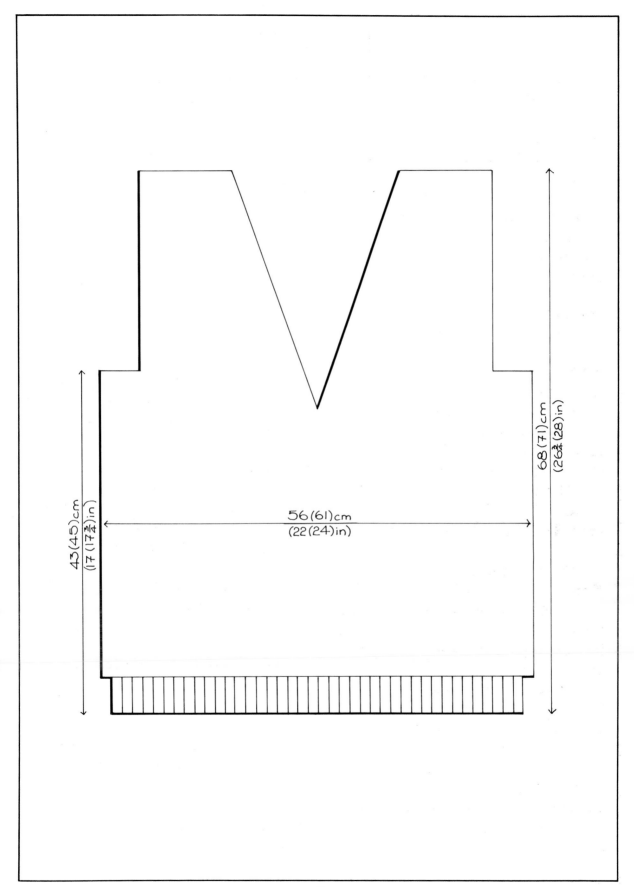

56(61)cm
(22(24)in)

43(45)cm
(17(17¾)in)

68(71)cm
(26¾(28)in)

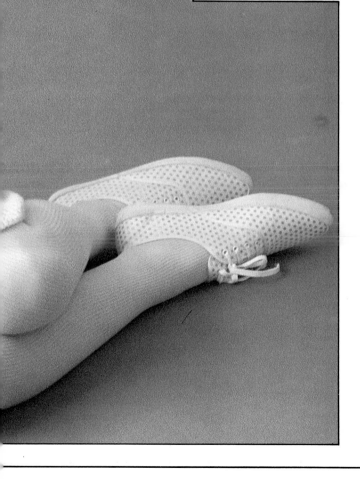

PASTEL POWER

PASTEL POWER

A natty sweater dress with unusual contrasting cuffs and collar.

MATERIALS

19 (19, 20) 50g balls Scheepjeswol Superwash Zermatt in main colour **(M)**; 2 balls in 1st contrast colour **(A)**; 1 ball in 2nd contrast colour **(B)** and 1 ball in 3rd contrast colour **(C)**. Pair each 3¼mm and 4mm knitting needles. 3 buttons.

MEASUREMENTS

To fit 86 (91, 96)cm (34 (36, 38)in) bust; length from shoulder 96 (98, 100)cm (38 (38½, 39¼)in); sleeve seam 44 (45, 46)cm (17¼ (17½, 18)in). Figures in brackets refer to larger sizes.

TENSION

22 sts and 30 rows to 10cm (4in) over st-st on 4mm needles.

BACK

Using 3¼mm needles and A cast on 118 (124, 130) sts and work 8 cm (3¼in) in K1, P1 rib. Change to 4mm needles and M and cont in st-st until work measures 70 (71, 72)cm (27½ (28, 28¼)in) from cast-on edge, mark each end of row with contrast thread. Cont in st-st until work measures 96 (98, 100)cm (38 (38½, 39¼)in) from cast-on edge, ending with a P row.

Shape Shoulders: cast off 21 (22, 23) sts at beg of next 4 rows. Leave rem 34 (36, 38) sts on a holder.

FRONT

Work as for back until work measures 75 (77, 79)cm (29½ (30¼, 31)in) from cast-on edge, ending with a wrong side row.

Divide for Neck Opening: K56 (59, 62) sts, cast off 6 sts, K to end. Cont on these sts for right side, leave rem sts on spare needle. Cont straight in st-st until work measures 14cm (5½in), ending at neck edge.

Shape Neck: cast off 4 (5, 6) sts at beg of next row, cast off 3 sts at beg of foll alternate row, 2 sts at beg of next

alternate row and one st at beg of every foll alt row until 42 (44, 46) sts rem. Cont straight until work measures same as back to shoulder, ending at side edge.

Shape Shoulders: cast off 21 (22, 23) sts at beg of next row. Work one row. Cast off rem 21 (22, 23) sts. Rejoin yarn to sts on spare needle. Complete left side as for right side, reversing shapings.

LEFT SLEEVE

Using 3¼mm needles and B, cast on 48 (50, 50) sts and work 8cm (3¼in) in K1, P1 rib, inc 10 (10, 12) sts evenly across last row. 58 (60, 62) sts. Change to 4mm needles and M and cont in st-st, inc one st at each end of every foll 3rd row until there are 116 (120, 124) sts. Cont straight in st-st until sleeve seam measures 44 (45, 46)cm (17¼ (17½, 18)in) from cast-on edge, ending with a P row. Cast off.

RIGHT SLEEVE

Work as for left sleeve, but work cuff in A.

BUTTON BAND

Using 3¼mm needles and A, pick up and K 38 sts down left side neck opening and work 12 rows in K1, P1 rib. Cast off in rib.

BUTTONHOLE BAND

Using 3¼mm needles and B, pick up and K 38 sts up right side neck opening and work 5 rows in K1, P1 rib.
1st buttonhole row: rib 6, *cast off 2, rib 10 (including st already on needle); repeat from * to end, ending last repeat rib 6.
2nd buttonhole row: rib to end, casting on 2 sts over those cast off.
Rib 5 more rows. Cast off in rib.

COLLAR

Join shoulder seams. Using 3¼mm needles and C, pick up and K 30 sts up right front neck edge, K 34 (36, 38) sts across back, pick up and K 30 sts down left front neck edge.

94 (96, 98) sts. Work 4cm (1½in) in K1, P1 rib.
Inc row: rib 10 (11, 12) sts, *inc into next st; rep from *73 times, rib to end. 168 (170, 172) sts. Work straight in rib for a further 6cm (2¼in). Cast off in rib.

TO MAKE UP

Lap buttonhole band over button band and sew in place at base of opening. Sew in sleeves, placing centre of sleeves to shoulder seams. Join side and sleeve seams. Sew on buttons.

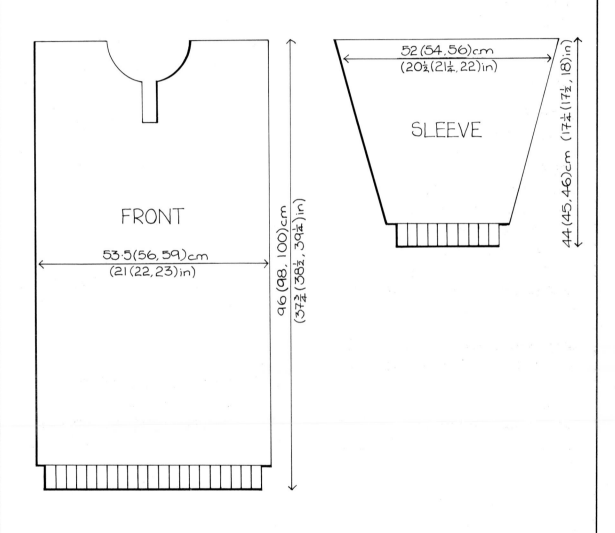

FRONT

53·5(56, 59)cm
(21(22,23)in)

96(98, 100)cm
(37¾(38½, 39¼)in)

52(54, 56)cm
(20½(21¼, 22)in)

SLEEVE

44(45,46)cm (17¼(17½, 18)in)

PURPLE IN

MOTION

PURPLE IN MOTION

A sporty, raglan sleeved two-tone jacket using garter stitch and stocking stitch. Perhaps you could knit this in just one colour, or how about stripes?

MATERIALS

9 (10, 10) 50g balls W.H. Smith Pure Wool Chunky in colour **(A)**; 8 (9, 10) balls in colour **(B)**. Pair each 4mm and 5mm knitting needles. 6 snap fasteners.

MEASUREMENTS

To fit 81-86 (91-96; 102-107)cm (32-34 (36-38; 40-42)in) bust; length 60 (63, 66)cm (23½ (24¾, 26)in); sleeve seam 38 (40, 42)cm (15 (16, 16¾)in). Figures in brackets refer to larger sizes.

TENSION

18 sts and 22 rows to 10cm (4in) over st-st on 5mm needles.

BACK

Using 4mm needles and A cast on 85 (89, 93) sts.
1st row: P1, *K1, P1; rep from * to end.
2nd row: K1, *P1, K1; rep from * to end.
Rep these 2 rows for 6cm (2½in), ending with a 1st rib row.
Next row: rib 2 (4, 6) sts, * inc in next st, rib 7; rep from * to last 3 (5, 7) sts, inc in next st, rib to end. 96 (100, 104) sts.
Change to 5mm needles and B. Beginning with a K row work in st-st until work measures 36 (38, 40)cm (14 (15, 15¾)in) from cast-on edge, ending with a P row.

Shape Raglan Armholes: cast off 3 sts at beg of next 2 rows, 2 sts at beg of next 8 rows. Dec one st at each end of every foll alternate row until 32 (34, 36) sts rem. Cast off.

LEFT FRONT

Using 4mm needles and A cast on 41 (43, 45) sts. Work 6cm (2½in) in rib as set on back, ending with a 1st rib row.
Next row: rib 2 (3, 4) sts, * inc in next st, rib 5; rep from * to last 3 (4, 5) sts, inc in next st, rib to end. 48 (50, 52) sts.
Change to 5mm needles and B. Beg with a K row work in

st-st until work measures 36 (38, 40)cm (14 (15, 15¾)in) from cast-on edge, ending at armhole edge.

Shape Raglan Armhole: cast off 3 sts at beg of next row, 2 sts at beg of foll 4 alternate rows. Dec one st at beg of every foll alternate row until 25 (26, 27) sts rem, ending at neck edge.

Shape Neck: cast off 7 sts at beg of next row and dec one st at end of this row. Work one row.
Cast off 3 sts at beg of next row and dec one st at end of this row. Work one row.
Cast off 2 sts at beg of next row and dec one st at end of this row.
Rep last 2 rows once. Work one row.
Dec one st at each end of next row and foll alternate row.
Cont to dec one st at raglan edge on every alternate row until 0 (1, 2) sts rem. Fasten off (fasten off, cast off 2 sts).

RIGHT FRONT

Work as for left front reversing shaping.

Sleeves (worked entirely in A).
Using 4mm needles cast on 43 (45, 47) sts. Work 6cm (2½in) in rib as set on back, ending with a 1st rib row.
Next row: rib 3 (4, 3) sts, * inc in next st, rib 5 (5, 4) sts; rep from * to last 4 (5, 4) sts, inc in next st, rib to end. 50 (52, 56) sts. Change to 5mm needles and work in garter st (every row K) throughout. K2 rows. Inc one st at each end of next and every foll 7th row until there are 74 (78, 82) sts. K4 (2, 4) rows straight.

Shape Raglan Armholes: cast off 3 sts at beg of next 2 rows, 2 sts at beg of foll 8 rows. Dec one st at each end of every foll alternate row until 10 (12, 14) sts rem. Cast off.

FRONT BORDERS (both alike)

Using 4mm needles and A cast on 9 sts. Work 6cm (2½in) in rib as set on back. Change to B and cont in rib until border, when slightly stretched, fits up front edge. Cast off. Stitch borders into position.

COLLAR

Using 4mm needles and A cast on 33 (35, 37) sts. Work one row in rib as set on back. Cont in rib, cast on 5 sts at beg of next 6 rows, 4 sts at beg of foll 12 rows and 2 sts at beg of next 4 (4, 6) rows. 119 (121, 127) sts. Cont in rib until work measures 10cm (4in) at centre from original cast-on edge. Cast off in rib.

TO MAKE UP

Join raglan seams. Join side and sleeve seams. Set in collar. Position snap fasteners evenly along front borders.

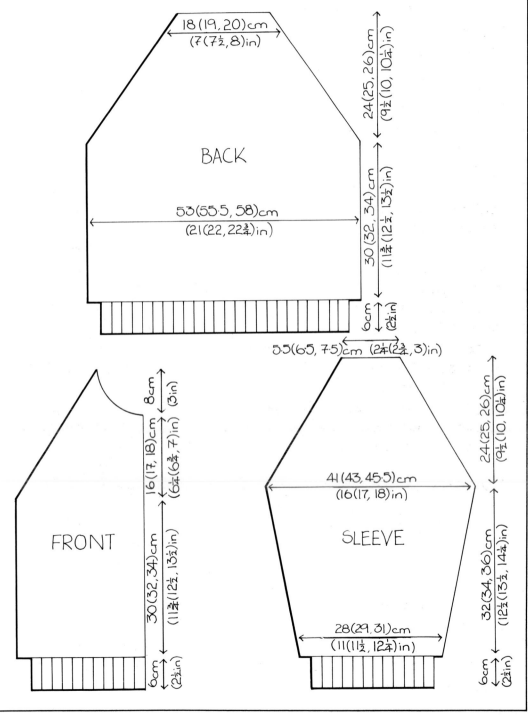

49

CHECK

MATE

CHECKMATE

This chunky checked jacket with effectively striped welts and shawl collar will knit up super-fast on large needles.

MATERIALS

12 (13) 50g balls Wendy Shetland Chunky in black **(B)**; 10 (11) balls in white **(W)**. Pair 5½mm and pair extra long 6½mm or circular 6½mm knitting needles. 4 buttons; 4 press studs.

MEASUREMENTS

To fit 86-91 (96-102)cm (34-36 (38-40)in) bust; length from shoulder 55 (57)cm (21¼ (22½)in); sleeve seam 46cm (18in) for both sizes. Figures in brackets refer to larger size.

TENSION

16 sts and 22 rows to 10cm (4in) over patt on 6½mm needles.

NOTE

The jacket is knitted from side to side, starting at right cuff.

RIGHT SLEEVE

Using 5½mm needles and B cast on 42 (46) sts. Work in stripe rib patt as follows.
1st row: using B, *K1, P1; rep from * to end.
2nd row: as 1st row.
3rd row: using W, as 1st row.
4th row: as 3rd row.
Rep these 4 rows until work measures 10cm (4in) from cast-on edge, inc 11 (13) sts evenly across last row. 53 (59) sts. Change to 6½mm needles and work as follows.
1st row (right side): using B, K to end.
2nd row: using B, P to end.
3rd row: using W, * K2, sl 1; rep from * to last 2 sts, K2.
4th row: using W, * P2, sl 1 purlwise; rep from * to last 2 sts, P2.

These 4 rows set the patt. Repeat them another 19 times, AT THE SAME TIME inc one st at each end of next and every foll 3rd row until there are 103 (107) sts.

Shape Right Side Front: cont in patt, cast on 38 (39) sts at beg of next 2 rows. 179 (185) sts. Cont in patt work a further 38 (42) rows straight, but knit the first and last 2 sts of every row to form selvedge edge.

Shape Neck: cont in patt, cast off 90 (93) sts at beg of next row. Cont on rem 89 (92) sts for a further 41 rows, omitting to work selvedge on back neck edge.

Shape Left Side Front: cont in patt, cast on 90 (93) sts at beg of next row. Work a further 37 (39) rows, working selvedge edges as before. Cast off 38 (39) sts at beg of next row.

Left Sleeve: patt 3 rows. Dec one st at each end of next and every foll 3rd row until 53 (59) sts rem. Patt 4 rows, dec 11 (13) sts evenly across last row. 42 (46) sts. Change to 5½mm needles and work in stripe rib patt as on right sleeve. Cast off in rib.

COLLAR AND CENTRE FRONT

Using 6½mm circular needle and B, with right side facing pick up and K 90 (93) sts up right side front, 34 sts across back neck, pick up and K 90 (93) sts down left side front. 214 (220) sts. Work 20cm (8in)in stripe rib patt as before, ending with black. Cast off in rib.

TO MAKE UP

Join side and sleeve seams. Lap right side front rib over left side rib. Sew 2 buttons at each edge of right side rib and 2 buttons above these, sew press studs to correspond behind buttons and left side rib.

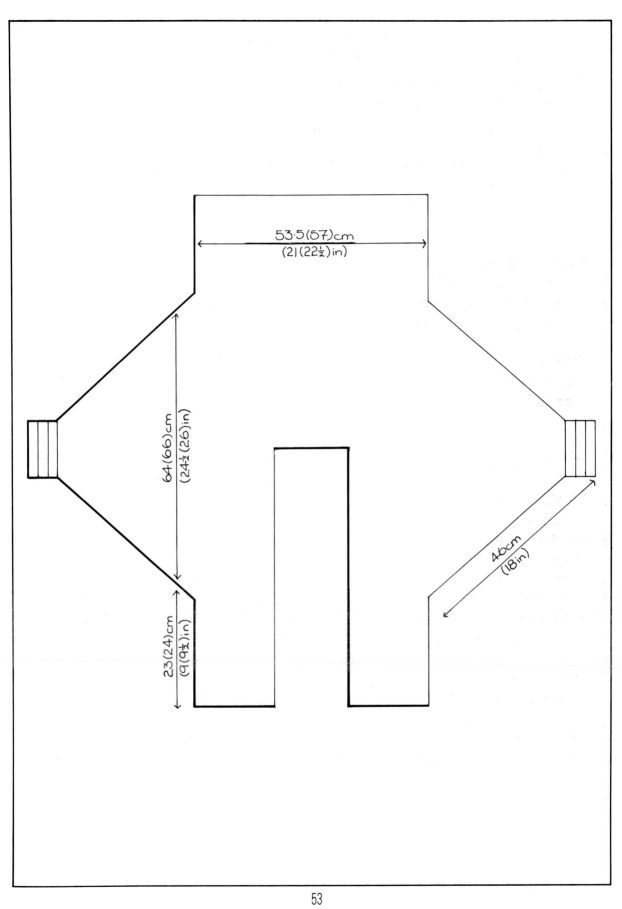

53.5(57)cm
(21(22½)in)

64(66)cm
(24½(26)in)

23(24)cm
(9(9½)in)

46cm
(18in)

COUNTRY
TWEED

COUNTRY TWEED

Weighty and warm — the wrap over collar is deep and the whole is knitted using the wool double throughout. A true rustic look so right for the country.

MATERIALS

18 (19, 20) 50g balls Rowan Fleck DK. Pair of 5mm knitting needles.

MEASUREMENTS

To fit 81-86 (91-96; 102-107)cm (32-34 (36-38; 40-42)in) bust; length from shoulder 59.5 (60, 62)cm (23¼ (23½, 24¼)in); sleeve seam 29.5 (31, 32)cm (11½ (12¼, 12½)in). Figures in brackets refer to larger sizes.

TENSION

18 sts and 24 rows to 10cm (4in) over patt on 5mm needles.

BACK

Cast on 85 (89, 93) sts. Work in sand stitch patt as follows.
1st row (wrong side): K.
2nd row: *K1, P1; rep from * to last st, K1.
These 2 rows form patt. Cont in patt, inc one st at each end of next row and every foll 3rd row until there are 123 (127, 131) sts. Patt 3 (3, 5) rows straight.

Shape Raglan Armholes: (wrong side facing), cast off 6 sts at beg of next 2 rows, 3 sts at beg of foll 2 rows and 2 sts at beg of next 2 rows. Dec one st at each end of every foll alternate row until 47 (49, 51) sts rem. Patt 2 rows**. Dec one st at each end of next row and every foll 3rd row until 39 (41, 43) sts rem. Patt 4 rows straight, thus ending with a right side row.

Shape Neck: still keeping raglan edge straight, patt 12 (13, 13) sts and slip these onto a holder for left back neck, cast off next 15 (15, 17) sts, patt to end. Work on the last set of 12 (13, 13) sts for right back neck. Patt one row. Cast off 4 sts at beg of next row. Rep last 2 rows once. Patt one row. Cast off rem 4 (5, 5) sts. Rejoin yarn to sts on holder and work to match right back neck reversing shaping.

FRONT

Work as given for back to **. 47 (49, 51) sts. Dec one st at each end of next row, patt 2 rows straight. Dec one st at each end of next row.

Shape Neck: patt 16 (17, 18), slip these sts onto a holder for left front neck, cast off next 11 sts, patt to end. Work on last set of 16 (17, 18) sts for right front neck. Patt one row. Cast off 3 (3, 4) sts at beg of next row and dec one st at end of this row for raglan shaping. Patt one row. Cast off 2 sts at beg of next row. Dec one st at beg of next row.
Cast off 2 sts at beg of next row. Patt one row.
Dec one st at neck edge on next row and foll 2 alternate rows. Patt 3 rows straight.
Cast off rem 4 (5, 5) sts. Rejoin yarn to sts on holder and work to match right front neck, reversing shaping.

SLEEVES

Cast on 51 (53, 55) sts. Work in patt as set on back, inc one st at each end of 3rd row and every foll 3rd row until there are 97 (101, 105) sts. Patt 1 (1, 2) rows straight, thus ending with a right side row.

Shape Raglan Armholes: cast off 6 sts at beg of next 2 rows, 3 sts at beg of foll 2 rows and 2 sts at beg of next 2 rows. Dec one st at each end of every foll alt row until 21 (23, 25) sts rem. Patt 2 rows. Dec one st at each end of next row and every foll 3rd row until 15 (17, 19) sts rem. Patt 2 rows. Cast off.

RAGLAN EDGING

With right side of work facing, pick up and K 84 sts along one raglan edge. Work 2 rows in K1, P1 rib. Cast off in rib. Work 3 other raglan edges in the same way.

COLLAR

Cast on 23 sts.
1st row: *K1, P1; rep from * to last st, K1.
Cont in rib, cast on 5 sts at beg of next 4 rows, 4 sts at beg

of next 12 rows and 2 sts at beg of next 6 (6, 8) rows. 103 (103, 107) sts. Rib 2 rows. Cast off in rib.

TO MAKE UP

Join raglan seams. Join side and sleeve seams. Set in collar, overlapping right over left.

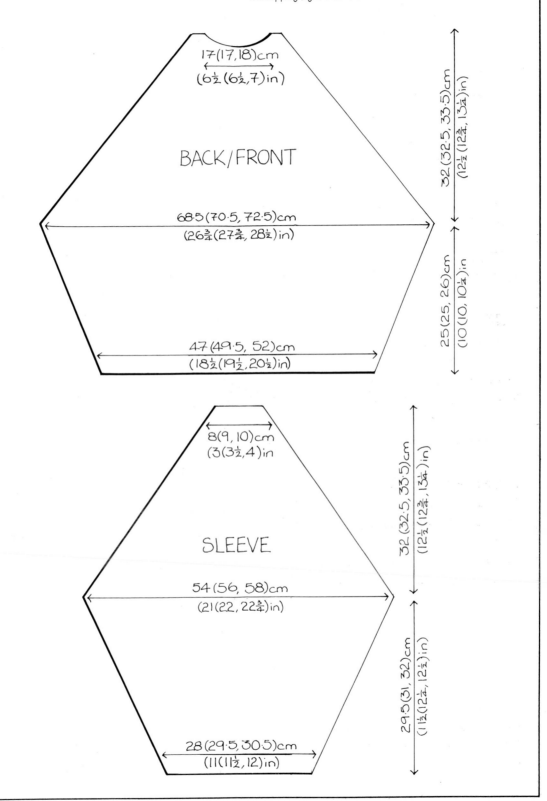

17 (17, 18) cm
($6\frac{1}{2}$ ($6\frac{1}{2}$, 7) in)

BACK / FRONT

68.5 (70.5, 72.5) cm
($26\frac{3}{4}$ ($27\frac{3}{4}$, $28\frac{1}{2}$) in)

47 (49.5, 52) cm
($18\frac{1}{2}$ ($19\frac{1}{2}$, $20\frac{1}{2}$) in)

32 (32.5, 33.5) cm
($12\frac{1}{2}$ ($12\frac{3}{4}$, $13\frac{1}{4}$) in)

25 (25, 26) cm
(10 (10, $10\frac{1}{4}$) in)

8 (9, 10) cm
(3 ($3\frac{1}{2}$, 4) in)

SLEEVE

54 (56, 58) cm
(21 (22, $22\frac{3}{4}$) in)

28 (29.5, 30.5) cm
(11 ($11\frac{1}{2}$, 12) in)

32 (32.5, 33.5) cm
($12\frac{1}{2}$ ($12\frac{3}{4}$, $13\frac{1}{4}$) in)

29.5 (31, 32) cm
($11\frac{1}{2}$ ($12\frac{1}{4}$, $12\frac{1}{2}$) in)

SNAPPY STRIPES

SNAPPY STRIPES

Be bold with this long-line, double breasted jacket with a striking collar.

MATERIALS

17 (19) 50g balls W.H. Smith Chunky Pure Wool in jade **(J)**, 3 balls each of cream **(C)** and black **(B)**. Pair each 4½mm and 5mm knitting needles. 4 buttons.

MEASUREMENTS

To fit 81-91 (96-107)cm (32-36 (38-42)in) bust; length from shoulder 71 (76)cm (28 (30)in); sleeve seam 38 (40)cm (15 (15¾)in). Figures in brackets refer to larger size.

TENSION

18 sts and 22 rows to 10cm (4in) over st-st on 5mm needles.

BACK

Using 4½mm needles and J cast on 97 (106) sts. Work 2cm (¾in) in K1, P1 rib, increasing one st at each end of last row. 99 (108) sts. Change to 5mm needles. Beg with a K row work straight in st-st until work measures 41 (44)cm (16 (17½)in), mark each end of next row with a contrast thread for start of armhole. Cont straight until work measures 28 (30)cm (11 (11¾)in) from marker, ending with a P row.

Shape Neck: K42 (45) and slip these sts onto a holder for right back neck, cast off next 15 (18) sts and K to end. P1 row.
Cast off 6 sts at beg of next row. P1 row.
Cast off rem 36 (39) sts. Rejoin yarn to sts on holder and complete to match left back neck.

LEFT FRONT

Using 4½mm needles and J cast on 62 (67) sts. Work 2cm (¾in) in K1, P1 rib, increasing one st at end of last row. 63 (68) sts. Change to 5mm needles and work as follows.
1st row: K to last 6 sts, * P1, K1; rep from * to end.

2nd row: *P1, K1; rep from * twice, P to end.
Rep these 2 rows until work measures 26 (29) cm (10¾ (11½) in) ending with a P row.

Shape Neck: K to last 6 sts, slip these 6 sts onto a safety pin for front border. Dec one st at beg of next row and every foll 4th row until 36 (39) sts rem. Cont straight until work measures same as back to shoulder. Cast off.

RIGHT FRONT

Work as for left front reversing all shaping, but work buttonholes when work measures 5cm (2in) as follows: with right side facing, rib 5 sts, cast off 2 sts, K to end. On foll row cast on 2 sts over those cast off. Work 2nd buttonhole when work measures 21cm (8¼in).

SLEEVES

Using 4½mm needles and J cast on 55 (59) sts.
1st row: K1, *P1, K1; rep from * to end.
2nd row: P1, *K1, P1; rep from * to end.
Rep these 2 rows for 2cm (¾in). Change to 5mm needles.
Work 2 rows in st-st. Cont in st-st, inc one st at each end of next and every foll 3rd row until there are 107 (115) sts.
Work 2 rows. Cast off.

COLLAR

Using 4½mm needles and with wrong side facing take 6 sts from safety pin on right front border and work in stripe rib pattern of 22 rows B and 22 rows W throughout, AT THE SAME TIME inc one st at beg of first row and every foll alternate row until there are 61 sts. Work 66 rows straight in stripe pattern, then dec one st on every alternate row at seam edge until 6 sts rem. Slip these onto a safety pin.

TO MAKE UP

Stitch collar into position. Graft 6 sts on safety pin from collar to 6 sts on safety pin from left front border. Set in sleeves between markers. Join side and sleeve seams. Sew on buttons.

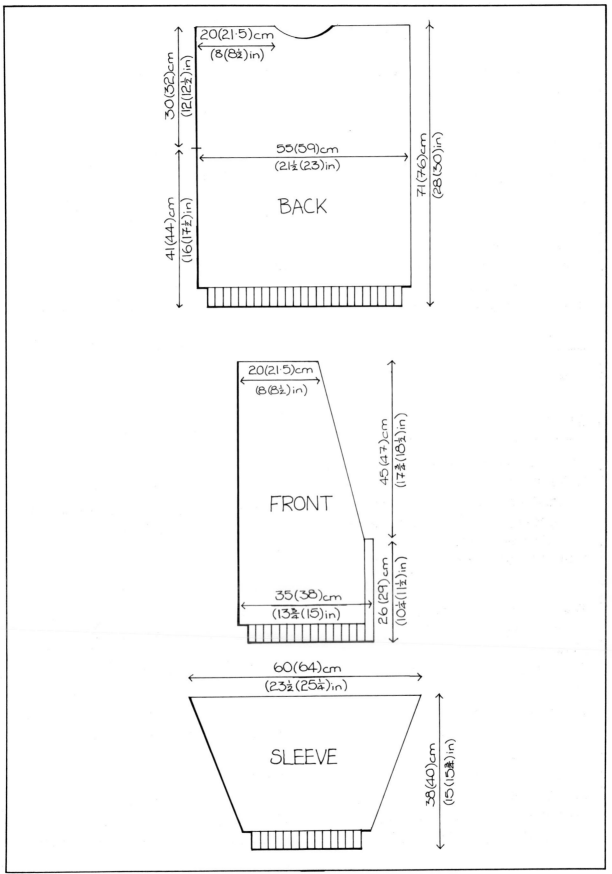

BACK

20(21.5)cm
(8(8½)in)

30(32)cm
(12(12½)in)

55(59)cm
(21½(23)in)

71(76)cm
(28(30)in)

41(44)cm
(16(17½)in)

FRONT

20(21.5)cm
(8(8½)in)

45(47)cm
(17¾(18½)in)

35(38)cm
(13¾(15)in)

26(29)cm
(10¼(11½)in)

SLEEVE

60(64)cm
(23½(25¼)in)

38(40)cm
(15(15¾)in)

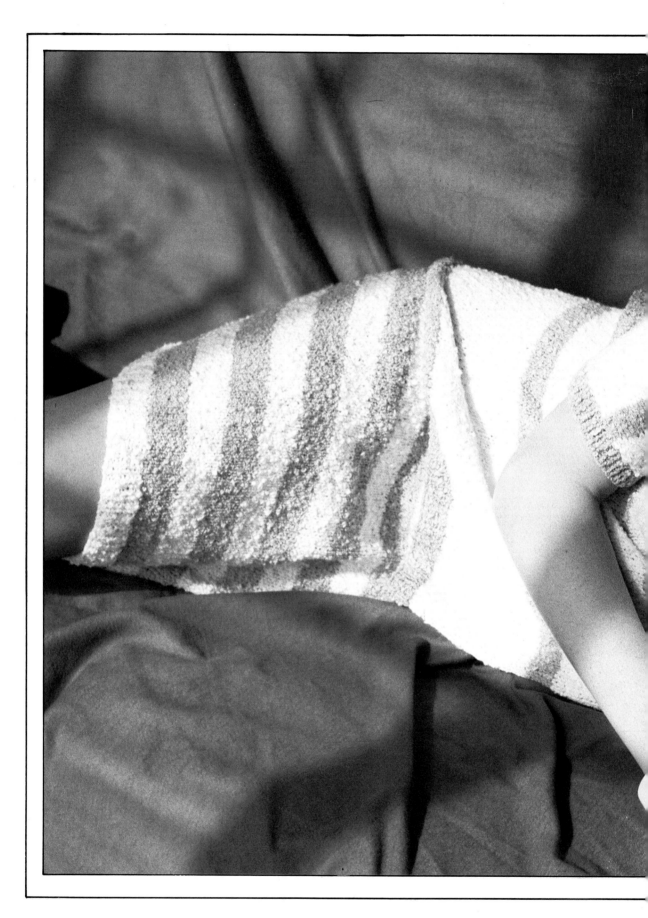

ALL STRIPED UP

ALL STRIPED UP

A cool and elegant striped tunic and skirt using textured yarns. For a longer skirt just add more stripes.

MATERIALS

Tunic: 7 (8) 50g balls Wendy Capri in white **(W)** and 3 (4) balls in green **(G)**.

Skirt: 3 (4) balls in white and 3 (4) balls in green. Waist length of 2.5cm (1in) wide elastic. Pair each 3¾mm and 4mm knitting needles.

MEASUREMENTS

Tunic: to fit 81-91 (96-107)cm (32-36 (38-42)in) bust; length from back neck 74.5 (79)cm (29¼ (31)in).

Skirt: to fit 86-91 (96-102)cm (34-36 (38-40)in) hips; length 49 (51)cm (19¼ (20)in). Figures in brackets refer to larger size.

TENSION

20 sts and 26 rows to 10cm (4in) over st-st on 4mm needles.

TUNIC BACK

Using 3¾mm needles and G, cast on 101 (111) sts.

1st row: K1, *P1, K1; rep from * to end.

2nd row: P1, *K1, P1; rep from * to end.

Rep these 2 rows twice more. Change to 4mm needles. Work in st-st and stripe pattern of 30 (32) rows W and 6 rows G. Rep these 36 (38) rows throughout, AT THE SAME TIME, inc one st at each end of every 9th (10th) row until there are 121 (131) sts to shape tunic. Work 10 (6) rows straight.

Shape Sleeve: cont in st-st and stripe pattern, cast off 5 sts at beg of next 8 rows. 161 (171) sts. Cont straight for a further 66 (70) rows **.

Shoulder and Neck Shapings: working with G only, cont in st-st, leave 15 sts unworked at end of next 2 (4) rows, 13 sts at end of next 2 (0) rows and 5 (6) sts at end of next 4 rows, the last row was worked on 85 (87) sts.

Next row: K32 sts, leave these on a holder for right back, cast off next 21 (23) sts, K until there are 27 sts on right hand

needle after those cast off, turn, thus leaving 5 more sts unworked. Cont on these sts for left back.

P1 row. * Cast off 4 sts at beg of next row and leave 5 more sts unworked at end of row. P1 row*. Rep from * to * once. Cast off 4 sts at beg of next row. Place 58 (62) sts for left shoulder onto holder. Rejoin yarn to sts on holder and work to match left back, reversing shaping.

FRONT

Work as for back to **.

Shoulder and Neck Shapings: (with right side facing), working with G only, cont in st-st, K70 (74) sts, slip these onto a holder for left front, cast off next 21 (23) sts, K55 (59) sts, thus leaving 15 sts unworked. P1 row. Cast off 4 sts at beg of next row, K38 (40) sts leaving 13 (15) sts unworked.

P1 row. *Cast off 2 sts at beg of next row and leave 5 (6) sts unworked at end of row. P1 row*. Rep from * to * twice (once). For larger size only rep from * to * again but leave 5 not 6 sts unworked at end of row.

For both sizes, dec one st at beg of next row, K11 sts and turn leaving another 5 sts unworked. P1 row. Rep the last two rows once. Place rem 58 (62) sts on holder for right shoulder. Rejoin yarn to sts on holder and work to match right front reversing shaping.

NECKBAND

Using 3¾mm needles and G, with right side facing, pick up and K 49 (51) sts from back and 57 (59) sts from front. 106 (110) sts. Work 6 rows in K1, P1 rib. Cast off in rib.

TO MAKE UP

Hold the two groups of sts of right front and back together and, with P sides inside, graft together. Join left shoulder in same way. Using 3¾mm needles and G, with right side facing, pick up and K 110 (120) sts along outer edge of sleeve. Work 6 rows in K1, P1 rib. Cast off in rib. Work other sleeve border in same way.

Join all seams being careful to match stripes.

SKIRT (worked in one piece)

Using 3¾mm needles and W, cast on 200 (220) sts and work 8 rows in K1, P1 rib. Change to 4mm needles. Work in st-st and stripe pattern of 8 rows G and 8 rows W. Work these 16 rows 7 times. For larger size only work a further 8 rows in G. For both sizes, change to 3¾mm needles and work 6cm (2¼in) in K1, P1 rib using G (W). Cast off in rib.

TO MAKE UP

Join side seam matching stripes. Using the length of elastic join the ends to form a ring. Fold rib section at top of skirt in half to wrong side enclosing elastic and slip stitch into position.

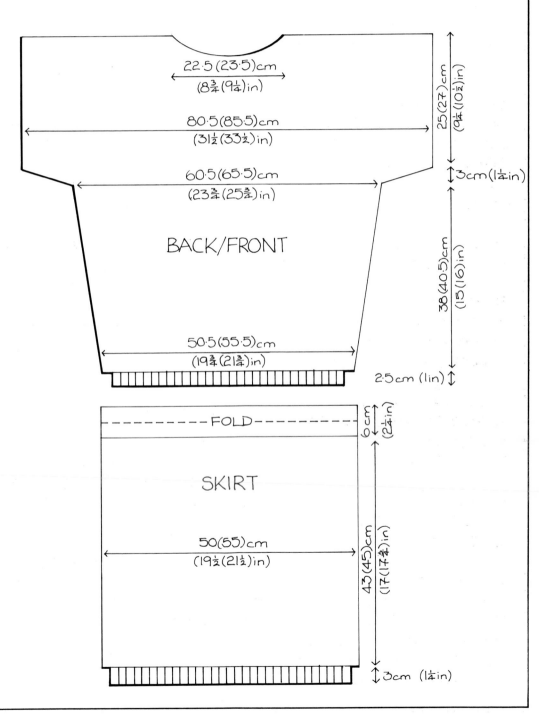

COTTON ON
COTTON ON
COTTON ON
COTTON ON

COTTON ON

Shirt neck cardigan with cutaway armholes in stocking stitch. Simple sophistication.

MATERIALS

6 (7, 8) 50g balls of Hayfield Raw Cotton DK. Pair each 3¼mm and 4mm knitting needles. 7 buttons.

MEASUREMENTS

To fit 81-86 (91-96, 102-107)cm (32-34 (36-38, 40-42)in) bust; length from shoulder 59 (61, 62.5)cm (23¼ (24, 24½)in). Figures in brackets refer to larger sizes.

TENSION

21 sts and 28 rows to 10cm (4in) over st-st on 4mm needles.

BACK

Using 3¼mm needles cast on 92 (96, 100) sts and work 7cm (2¾in) in K1, P1 rib.
Inc row: rib 2 (3, 2), * inc in next st, rib 10 (8, 7); rep from * to last 2 (3, 2) sts, inc in next st, rib to end. 101 (107, 113) sts. Change to 4mm needles and work in st-st until work measures 33 (34, 35)cm (13 (13½, 13¾)in), ending with a P row.

Shape Armholes: cast off 3 sts at beg of next 2 rows, 2 sts at beg of foll 4 (6, 8) rows, then dec one st at each end of every foll alternate row 8 times, then at each end of every foll 3rd row 8 times, then at each end of every foll 4th row 6 times. 43 (45, 47) sts.

Shape Neck: K8 (9, 10) sts, cast off next 27 sts, K to end. Cont on last set of sts only for first side. Cast off 3 sts at beg of next row, then dec one st at neck edge on foll row. Cast off rem 4 (5, 6) sts for shoulder edge. Return to rem 8 (9, 10) sts, with wrong-side facing, rejoin yarn and P to end. Cont to match first side reversing shapings.

LEFT FRONT

Using 3¼mm needles cast on 45 (47, 49) sts and work 7cm (2¾in) in K1, P1 rib.

Inc row: rib 2 (3, 3), * inc in next st, rib 9 (7, 6); rep from * to last 3 (4, 4) sts, inc in next st, rib to end. 50 (53, 56) sts. Change to 4mm and work in st-st until work measures 33 (34, 35)cm (13 (13½, 13¾)in), ending with a P row (ending with a K row on right front).

Shape Armhole: cast off 3 sts at beg of next row, 2 sts at beg of foll 2 (3, 4) alt rows, then dec one st at beg of foll 8 alt rows, then at armhole edge on every foll 3rd row 8 times, then on every foll 4th row 3 times. Work 2 rows straight.

Shape Neck: cast off 9 sts at beg of next row, dec one st at beg of foll row, cast off 4 sts at beg of foll row. Work one row straight.
Cast off 2 sts at beg of next row, then dec one st at beg of foll 2 rows. Work one row straight.
Dec one st at beg of next 2 rows. 4 (5, 6) sts. Work a few rows straight, until work measures same as back to shoulder. Cast off.

RIGHT FRONT

Work to match left front reversing all shaping.

COLLAR

Using 3¼mm needles cast on 159 sts.
1st row: K1, *P1, K1; rep from * to end.
2nd row: P1, *K1, P1; rep from * to end.
Rep these 2 rows for 7.5cm (3in). Cast off 12 sts at beg of next 8 rows. Cast off rem 63 sts.

BUTTONBAND

Using 3¼mm needles cast on 11 sts. Work in rib as for collar until, when slightly stretched, band fits up centre front edge. Cast off. Mark position of buttons on buttonband with pins – 1st, 1cm (½in) from cast-on edge; 2nd, in line with top of front ribbed welt; 3rd, 1cm (½in) from top of neck edge and rem 4 spaced equally between.

BUTTONHOLE BAND

Work as given for buttonband, working buttonholes when pin

positions are reached as follows.

1st row: rib 4, cast off 3, rib to end.

2nd row: rib to end, casting on 3 over those cast off.

ARMHOLE BORDERS

Join shoulder seams. Using 3¼mm needles and with right side facing, pick up and K 110 (118, 120) sts around armhole edge. Work in K1, P1 rib for 4 rows. Cast off in rib.

TO MAKE UP

Sew front bands into position. Sew cast-off edge of collar to neck edge. Join side seam and ends of borders. Press lightly on wrong side. Sew on buttons.

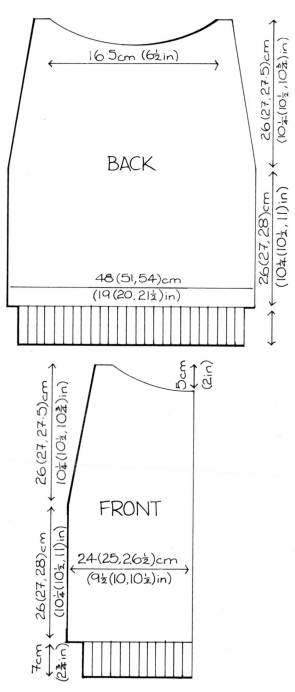

BACK

16.5cm (6½in)

26 (27, 27.5)cm (10¼ (10½, 10¾)in)

26 (27, 28)cm (10¼ (10½, 11)in)

48 (51, 54)cm (19 (20, 21½)in)

FRONT

24 (25, 26½)cm (9½ (10, 10½)in)

26 (27, 27.5)cm (10¼ (10½, 10¾)in)

26 (27, 28)cm (10¼ (10½, 11)in)

5cm (2in)

7cm (2¾in)

RANGE GRANDEUR

ORANGE GRANDEUR

A traditional shaped sweater with a snug, double ribbed polo neck.

MATERIALS

23 (24, 25) 25g hanks of Rowan lightweight DK. Pair each 3mm and 3¾mm knitting needles.

MEASUREMENTS

To fit 81-86 (91-96, 102-107)cm (32-34 (36-38, 40-42)in) bust; length from shoulder 65 (68, 71)cm (25½ (26¾, 28)in); sleeve seam 42 (43, 44)cm (16½ (17, 17¼)in). Figures in brackets refer to larger sizes.

TENSION

24 sts and 30 rows to 10cm (4in) over st-st on 3¾mm needles.

BACK

Using 3mm needles cast on 118 (122, 126) sts, work in double rib as follows.
1st row (right side): P2, *K2, P2; rep from * to end.
2nd row: K2, *P2, K2; rep from * to end. Rep these 2 rows until work measures 16cm (6¼in), ending with a 2nd row. Change to 3¾mm needles and work 2 rows in st-st. Cont in st-st inc one st at each end of next and every foll 6th row until there are 142 (148, 154) sts. Work 3 rows straight. Mark each end of row with a contrast thread for beg of armhole**. Cont straight until work measures 62 (65, 68)cm (24½ (25¾, 27)in), ending with a P row.

Shape Neck: K61 (63, 65) sts, slip these sts onto a holder, cast off next 20 (22, 24) sts, K to end. Work on last set of sts only for left back neck. P1 row.
Cast off 10 sts at beg of next row, 6 sts at beg of foll alternate row and 4 sts at beg of next alternate row. P1 row.
Cast off rem 41 (43, 45) sts. Rejoin yarn to sts on holder and complete to match left back neck.

FRONT

Work as given for back to **. Cont straight until work measures 57 (60, 63) cm (22½ (23½, 24¾) in).

Shape Neck: K61 (63, 65) sts, slip these sts onto a holder, cast off next 20 (22, 24) sts, K to end. P1 row.
Cast off 4 sts at beg of next row and foll 2 alternate rows, 2 sts at beg of next 2 alternate rows. Work one row.
Dec one st at beg of next row and 3 foll alternate rows. Work 5 rows.
Cast off rem 41 (43, 45) sts. Rejoin yarn to sts on holder and complete to match right side.

SLEEVES

Using 3mm needles cast on 62 (66, 70) sts. Work in rib as for back until work measures 8cm (3¼in), ending with a 1st row.
Next row: rib 1 (5, 9), inc in next st, * rib 5, inc in next st; rep from * to end. 73 (77, 81) sts. Change to 3¾mm needles and work 2 rows in st-st. Cont in st-st inc one st at each end of next and every foll 4th row until there are 123 (129, 135) sts. Work 3 rows straight. Cast off.

POLO COLLAR

Join right shoulder seam. Using 3mm needles and with right side facing, pick up and K32 down left front neck, 22 (24, 26) across centre front, 32 up right front neck, 12 sts down right back neck, 44 (46, 48) across centre back and finally 12 sts up left back neck. 154 (158, 162) sts. Work 19cm (7½in) in double rib as given on back. Cast off in rib.

TO MAKE UP

Join rem shoulder seam, carrying seam across collar reversing seam for turn back. Set in sleeves, placing centre of sleeves to shoulder seams. Join side and sleeve seams.

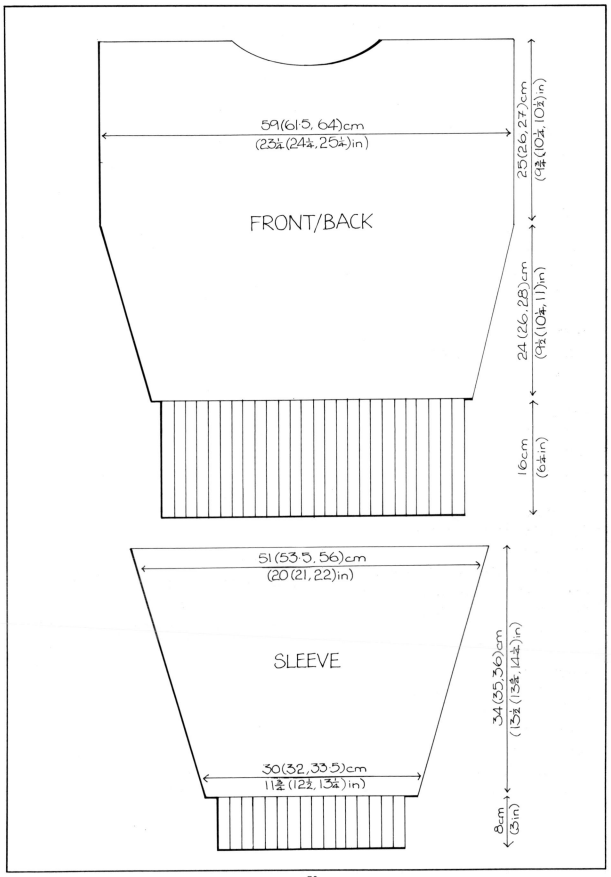

FRONT/BACK

59(61.5, 64)cm
(23¼(24¼, 25¼)in)

25(26, 27)cm
(9¾(10¼, 10½)in)

24(26, 28)cm
(9½(10¼, 11))in)

16cm
(6¼in)

SLEEVE

51(53.5, 56)cm
(20(21, 22)in)

30(32, 33.5)cm
11¾(12½, 13¼)in)

34(35, 36)cm
(13½(13¾, 14¼)in)

8cm
(3in)

PLUNGED IN GREEN

PLUNGED IN GREEN

An ample sweater worked in Irish moss stitch with a deep neck opening and shoulders emphasised with ribbing.

MATERIALS

20 (21, 22) 50g balls Sheepjeswol Superwash DK. Pair each 3¼mm and 4mm knitting needles and one 3¼mm circular needle.

MEASUREMENTS

To fit 81-86 (91-96, 102-107)cm (32-34 (36-38, 40-42)in) bust; length from shoulder 69 (72, 75)cm (27 (28¼, 29½)in); sleeve seam 56 (58, 60)cm (22 (22¾, 23½)in). Figures in brackets refer to larger sizes.

TENSION

22 sts and 28 rows to 10cm (4in) over patt on 4mm needles.

BACK

Using 4mm needles cast on 123 (129, 135) sts. Work in single rib as follows.

1st row: K1, *P1, K1: rep from * to end.

2nd row: P1, *K1, P1; rep from * to end.

Rep these 2 rows twice more. Now work in patt as follows.

1st row (right side): K1, *P1, K1; rep from * to end.

2nd and 3rd rows: P1, *K1; P1; rep from * to end.

4th row (wrong side): as 1st row.

These 4 rows form patt. Cont straight in patt until work measures 59 (62, 65)cm (23¼ (24½, 25½)in). Now work in single rib as set at beg of work for a further 10cm (4in). Cast off in rib.

FRONT

Work as given for back until work measures 23 (25, 27)cm (9 (9¾, 10½)in) from cast-on edge, ending with a wrong side row.

Neck Opening: patt 51 (53, 55) sts, place these sts on a holder for left front, cast off next 21 (23, 25) sts, patt to end. Work on this last set of sts for right front. Cont in patt, work 11 rows straight. Cont in patt, dec one st at neck edge on next row and every foll 12th row until 43 (45, 47) sts rem. Patt 4 (7, 10) rows straight. Now work in single rib as set at beg of back for a further 10cm (4in). Cast off in rib. Rejoin yarn to sts on holder and complete to match right front reversing shaping.

SLEEVES

Using 3¼mm needles cast on 89 (93, 97) sts. Work in single rib as set on back for 22cm (8¾in). Change to 4mm needles and work in patt as set on back until sleeve seam measures 36 (37, 38) cm (14¼ (14½, 15) in), ending with a wrong-side row. Inc one st at each end of next row and every foll 4th row until there are 115 (121, 127) sts. Patt 4 rows straight. Cast off.

COLLAR

Join shoulder seams. Using 3¼mm circular needle and with right side of work facing, pick up and K128 (131, 134) sts along right front opening, 37 (39, 41) sts across back neck and 128 (131, 134) sts down left front opening. 293 (301, 309) sts. Work 4 rows in single rib as set on back.

Inc row: rib 90 (93, 96) sts, * inc twice into next st, rib 3 sts; rep from * 30 times more, inc twice into next st, rib to end. 357 (365, 373) sts. Cont in rib until collar measures 10cm (4in). Cast off in rib.

TO MAKE UP

Sew collar to base of front opening, overlapping right over left. Set in sleeves, placing centre of sleeves to shoulder seams. Join side and sleeve seams.

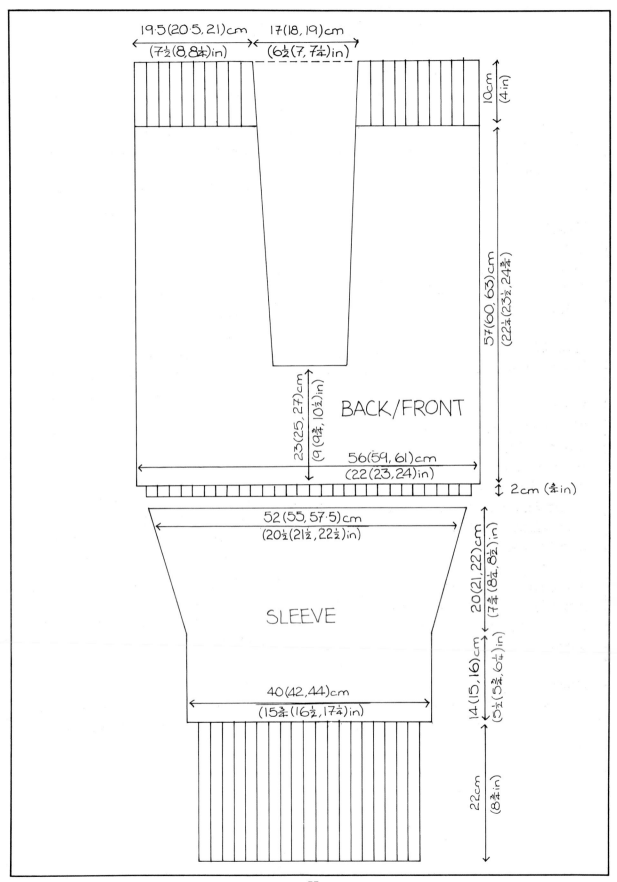

19.5(20.5, 21)cm
(7½(8, 8¾)in)

17(18, 19)cm
(6½(7, 7¾)in)

10cm
(4in)

57(60, 63)cm
(22¼(23½, 24¾)

BACK/FRONT

23(25, 27)cm
(9(9¾, 10½)in)

56(59, 61)cm
(22(23, 24)in)

2cm (¾in)

52(55, 57.5)cm
(20½(21½, 22½)in)

20(21, 22)cm
(7¾(8¼, 8½)in)

SLEEVE

14(15, 16)cm
(5½(5¾, 6¼)in)

40(42, 44)cm
(15¾(16½, 17¼)in)

22cm
(8¾in)

77

PURPLE PANACHE

PURPLE PANACHE

Long and sleeveless, this tunic is the ideal garment for those hot, summer days — a cool combination of lilac and white.

MATERIALS

6 (6, 7) 50g balls Pingouin Fil D'Ecosse No. 3 — white **(W)** and 6 (6, 7) balls in No. 33 — crocus **(C)**. Pair each 3¾mm and 4mm knitting needles. 9 snap fasteners.

MEASUREMENTS

To fit 81-86 (91-96, 102-107)cm (32-34 (36-38, 40-42)in) bust; length from shoulder 79 (82, 85)cm (31 (32¼, 33¼)in). Figures in brackets refer to larger sizes.

TENSION

21 sts and 29 rows to 10cm (4in) over st-st on 4mm needles.

NOTE

When changing colour twist tightly to prevent hole.

BACK

Using 3¾mm needles cast on as follows: 57 (60, 63) with C and 57 (60, 63) with W. Working in colours as set throughout, work 2cm (¾in) in K1, P1 rib. Change to 4mm needles and work straight in st-st until work measures 53 (55, 57) cm (20¼ (21½, 22½) in) from cast-on edge, ending with a P row.

Shape Armholes: cast off 6 sts at beg of next 2 rows, 4 sts at beg of foll 2 rows and 2 sts at beg of next 8 rows. Dec one st at each end of next alternate row and every foll alternate row until 56 (60, 64) sts rem. Cont straight until armhole measures 23 (24, 25) cm (9 (9½, 9¾) in), ending with a P row.

Shape Neck: K20 (21, 22), cast off next 16 (18, 20) sts, K to end. Work on last set of sts for left back neck.
P1 row. Cast off 4 sts at beg of next row. Rep from * to * twice. P1 row.
Cast off rem 8 (9, 10) sts. Rejoin yarn to rem 20 (21, 22) sts and work to match first side reversing shaping.

LEFT FRONT

Working with C only, using 3¾mm needles cast on 54 (57, 60) sts. Work 2cm (¾in) in rib as on back. Change to 4mm needles and work straight in st-st until work measures same as back to armholes, ending at armhole edge.

Shape Armhole: cast off 6 sts at beg of next row, 4 sts at beg of foll alternate row and 2 sts at beg of next 4 alternate rows, ending at neck edge.

Shape Neck: cast off 3 (4, 5) sts at beg of next row, dec one st at beg of foll row, cast off 2 sts at beg of next row, then dec one st at beg of each row 9 times. Cont to dec one st at armhole edge on every alternate row 5 (6, 7) times more and dec one st at neck edge on every 4th row 8 times. Cont straight on rem 8 (9, 10) sts until work measures same as back to cast off. Cast off.

RIGHT FRONT

Working with W only, work as for left front reversing shaping.

LEFT FRONT BAND

Using 3¾mm needles and C cast on 9 sts.
1st row: K1, *P1, K1; rep from * to end.
2nd row: P1, *K1, P1; rep from * to end.
Rep these 2 rows until band, when slightly stretched, fits up centre front edge to neck. Slip sts onto a safety pin.

RIGHT FRONT BAND

Working with W, work as for left front band.

LEFT ARMHOLE BORDER

Join side seams. Using 3¾mm needles and W, with right side facing, pick up and K156 (160, 164) sts around armhole.
Work 3 rows in K1, P1 rib.
Next row: rib to last 30 sts, turn and leave these sts unworked. Rep this row once.
Cont in rib leaving 5 sts at end of next 12 rows unworked. Cut yarn. Slip rem sts on left hand needle onto right hand needle and cast off in rib, ribbing every 4th and 5th st together.

RIGHT ARMHOLE BORDER

Working with C, work as for left armhole border.

NECKBAND

Join shoulder and armhole border seams. Slip sts from right front band onto 3¾mm needle and working with C and with right side facing, pick up and K82 (84, 86) sts up right front neck, 18 (19, 20) sts from shoulder to centre back, drop C, now using W, pick up and K18 (19, 20) from centre back to shoulder and 82 (84, 86) sts down left front neck, then rib 9 sts from left front band. Working in colours as set, work one row in rib. Cont in rib leaving 2 sts unworked at end of next 6 rows, cut yarn. Slip rem sts on left hand needle onto right hand needle, then cast off in rib, ribbing every 4th and 5th st together before casting off.

TO COMPLETE

Position snap fasteners evenly along front borders. Sew side seams and armhole border edges.

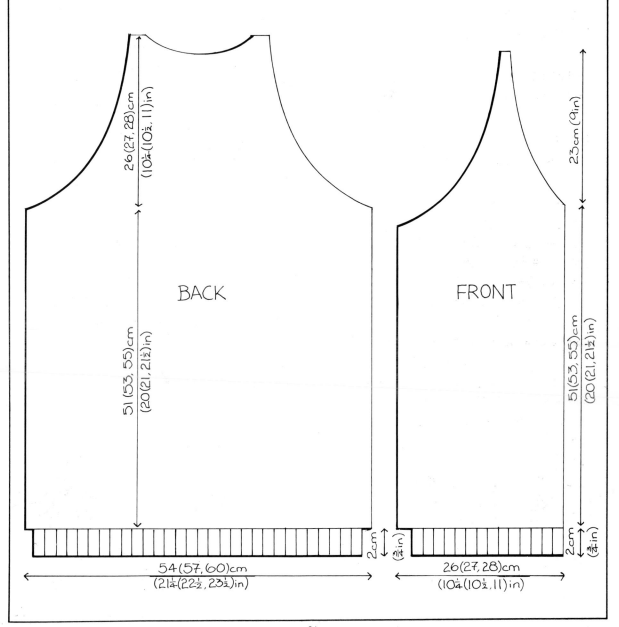

► BOW-BELLE ◄

BOW-BELLE

An easy-to-make striped top with a fun-to-wear bow tie.

MATERIALS

4 (4, 5) 50g balls Emu Cotton Perle in white **(W)**; 2 balls in black **(B)**. Pair each 3mm, 3¾mm and 2¾mm knitting needles.

MEASUREMENTS

To fit 86 (91, 96) cm (34 (36, 38) in) bust; length from shoulder 46 (47, 48) cm (18 (18½, 19) in). Figures in brackets refer to larger sizes.

TENSION

24 sts and 30 rows to 10cm (4in) over st-st on 3¾mm needles.

BACK

Using 3mm needles and W cast on 112 (120, 128) sts and work in K1, P1 rib, until work measures 3cm (1¼in) from cast-on edge. Change to 3¾mm needles. Beg with a K row work in st-st as follows: 2 rows B, 8 rows W. These 10 rows form patt and are rep throughout. Cont straight in patt until work measures 26cm (10¼in) from cast-on edge, ending with a P row.

Shape Armholes: cast off 8 (9, 10) sts at beg of next 2 rows. Cont in patt until work measures 46 (47, 48) cm (18 (18½, 19) in) from cast-on edge, ending with a P row.

Shape Shoulders: cast off 24 (26, 28) sts at beg of next 2 rows. Leave rem 48 (50, 52) sts on a holder.

FRONT

Work as given for back until work measures 39 (40, 41) cm (15½ (15¾, 16¼) in) from cast-on edge, ending with a P row.

Shape Neck: K32 (34, 36) sts, turn and leave rem sts on a spare needle. P1 row. Dec one st at neck edge on next and every foll alternate row until 24 (26, 28) sts rem. Cont straight in patt until work measures same as back to shoulder.

Shape Shoulders: cast off 24 (26, 28) sts. Return to sts on spare needle, slip centre 32 (34, 36) sts on a holder, rejoin yarn to rem 32 (34, 36) sts and K to end. Complete to match first side reversing shaping.

NECKBAND

Join right shoulder seam. Using 3mm needles and W pick up and K 22 sts down left front neck edge, K 32 (34, 36) sts across centre front, pick up and K 22 up right front neck edge and finally K across 48 (50, 52) sts at centre back neck. 124 (128, 132) sts. Work 2cm (¾in) in K1, P1 rib. Cast off in rib.

ARMBANDS

Join left shoulder seam. Using 3mm needles and W pick up and K100, (108, 116) sts evenly around armholes. Work 2cm (¾in) in K1, P1 rib. Cast off in rib.

BOW

Using 2¾mm needles and B, cast on 16 sts and work 20cm (8in) in st-st, ending with a P row. Cast off. Sew ends together. Using 2¾mm needles and B cast on 8 sts and work 6cm (2¼in) in st-st, ending with a P row. Cast off. Place large circle of knitting with seam at back, sew smaller circle ends together and place around centre of large one to form a bow. Sew to centre front neck.

TO MAKE UP

Join side and armband seams.

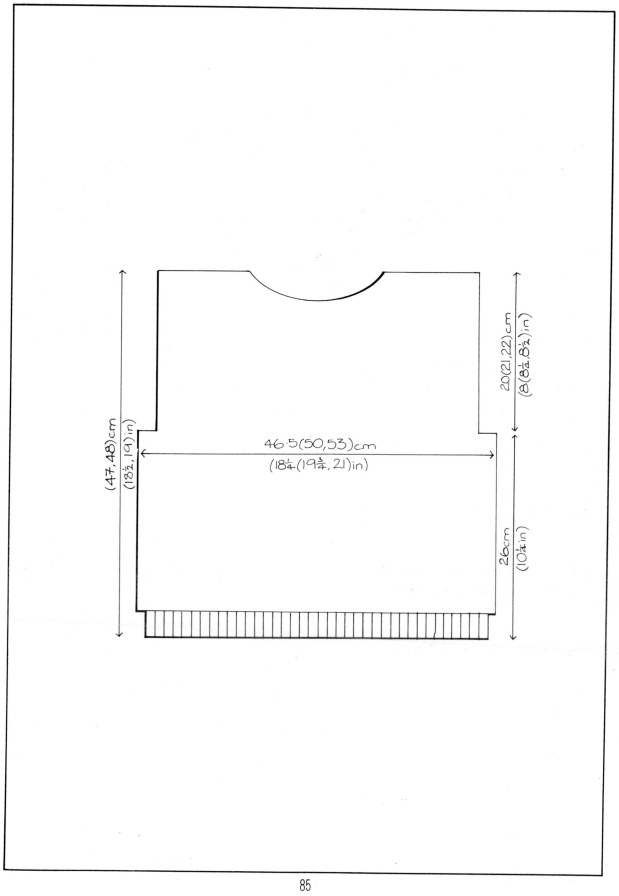

46.5(50,53)cm
(18¼(19¾, 21)in)

(47,48)cm
(18½,19)in

20(21,22)cm
(8(8¼,8½)in)

26cm
(10¼in)

HOLLYWOOD
SET

HOLLYWOOD SET

The yarn for this twin set is ribbon: glamorous and sparkling.

VEST

MATERIALS

9 (10, 11) 50g balls Pingouin Ruban. Pair each 4mm and 5½mm knitting needles.

MEASUREMENTS

To fit 81-86 (91-96, 102-107)cm (32-34 (36-38, 40-42)in) bust; length from shoulder 46 (48.5, 51)cm (18 (19, 20¼)in). Figures in brackets refer to larger sizes.

TENSION

17 sts and 24 rows to 10cm (4in) over st-st on 5½mm needles.

BACK

Using 4mm needles cast on 78 (84, 90) sts. Work 7cm (2¾in) in K1, P1 rib. Change to 5½mm needles. Beg with a K row work straight in st-st until work measures 29 (31, 33)cm (11¼ (12, 13)in) from cast-on edge, ending with a P row.

Shape Armholes: dec one st at each end of next and foll 19 (20, 21) alternate rows. Work one row. Cast off rem 38 (42, 46) sts loosely.

FRONT

Work as given for back until 32 (34, 36) rows of armhole shaping have been worked. 46 (50, 54) sts.

Shape Neck: K2 tog, work until there are 15 sts on right needle, slip these onto spare needle for left front, cast off next

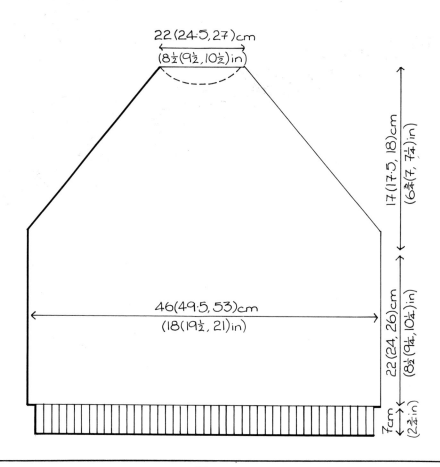

22 (24·5, 27)cm
(8½ (9½, 10½)in)

17 (17·5, 18)cm
(6¾ (7, 7¼)in)

46 (49·5, 53)cm
(18 (19½, 21)in)

22 (24, 26)cm
(8½ (9¼, 10¼)in)

7cm
(2¾in)

14 (18, 22), work to last 2 sts, K2 tog. Cont on these 15 sts for right front. Work one row. Cast off 4 sts at beg of next row, 3 sts at beg of foll alternate row and 2 sts on next alternate row and, AT THE SAME TIME, dec one st at armhole edge on every right side row 3 times. Work one row on rem 3 sts. Cast off. Rejoin yarn to neck edge of sts left on spare needle and complete to match right front.

TO MAKE UP AND BORDERS

Join left shoulder seam, the last 3 sts cast off on front shoulder to 3 sts at left side at upper edge of back, the same for right shoulder. Join side seams. Using 4mm needles and with right side facing, work around armhole as follows, picking up one st per row, K2 sts, * cast off one, pick up and K1; rep from * all around armhole. Work other armhole and then neck in the same way.

JACKET

MATERIALS

22 (23, 24) 50g balls Pingouin Ruban. Pair of 5½mm needles.

MEASUREMENTS

To fit 81-86 (91-96, 102-107)cm (32-34 (36-38, 40-42)in) bust; length from shoulder 47 (49, 51)cm (18½ (19¼, 20)in); sleeve seam 43 (44, 45)cm (17 (17¼, 17¾)in). Figures in brackets refer to larger sizes.

TENSION

17 sts and 24 rows to 10cm (4in) over st-st.

BACK

Cast on 70 (74, 78) sts and beg with a K row, work 13 rows in st-st.
Next row: P4 (3, 2) sts, (inc in next st, P2), 21 (23, 25) times, P to end. 91 (97, 103) sts. Beg with a P row cont straight in st-st until work measures 48 (50, 52)cm (19 (19¾, 20½)in) from cast-on edge, ending with a P row.

Shape Neck: K32 (34, 37), leave these sts on a holder for right back, cast off next 27 (29, 29) sts, K to end. Cont on rem 32 (34, 37) sts for left back. Work one row. Cast off 5

sts at beg of next row. P1 row. Cast off rem 27 (29, 32) sts. Rejoin yarn to rem 32 (34, 37) sts on holder cast off 5 sts, work to end. K1 row, and cast off.

RIGHT FRONT

Cast on 38 (41, 43) sts and beg with a K row, work 13 rows in st-st.
Next row: P2 (2, 1) sts, (inc in next st, P2) 12 (13, 14) times. 50 (54, 57) sts. Beg with a P row cont straight in st-st until work measures 42 (44, 46)cm (16½ (17¼, 18)in), from cast-on edge, ending at neck edge.

Shape Neck: cast off 9 (10, 10) sts at beg of next row, 5 (6, 6) sts at beg of foll alternate row, 3 sts on next alternate row, 2 sts on foll 2 alternate rows and one st on next 2 alternate rows. Cont on rem 27 (29, 32) sts until work measures same as back to shoulders. Cast off.

LEFT FRONT

Work as for right front, reversing all shaping.

SLEEVES

Cast on 38 (38, 40) sts and beg with a K row, work 13 rows in st-st.
Next row: P4 (4, 1) sts, (inc in next st, P2) 11 (11, 13) times, P1 (1, 0) sts. 49 (49, 53) sts. Beg with a P row work 2 rows in st-st. Cont in st-st inc, one st at each end of next row and every foll 4th row until there are 88 (91, 95) sts, then on every alternate row until there are 99 (99, 103) sts. Cont straight for 2 (3, 3) rows. Cast off.

NECKBAND

Join shoulder seams. With right side facing pick up and K61 (66, 66) sts all round neck edge. Beginning with a K row, work 13 rows in st-st. Cast off loosely.

RIGHT FRONT BAND

With right side facing, miss the first 7 rows at the beg of right front (this will be turned under for hem), pick up and K71 (73, 77) sts along front edge, leaving last 7 rows of neckband free. Work 13 rows in st-st. Cast off loosely.

LEFT FRONT BAND

Work as for right front band.

TO MAKE UP

Fold neck and front border in half to wrong side and slip stitch cast-off edges in place. Set in sleeves, placing centre of sleeves to shoulder seams. Join side and sleeve seams. Fold up 7 rows all round lower edge and sleeves and slip stitch cast-on edges in place on wrong side. Neaten top and bottom edges of front borders.

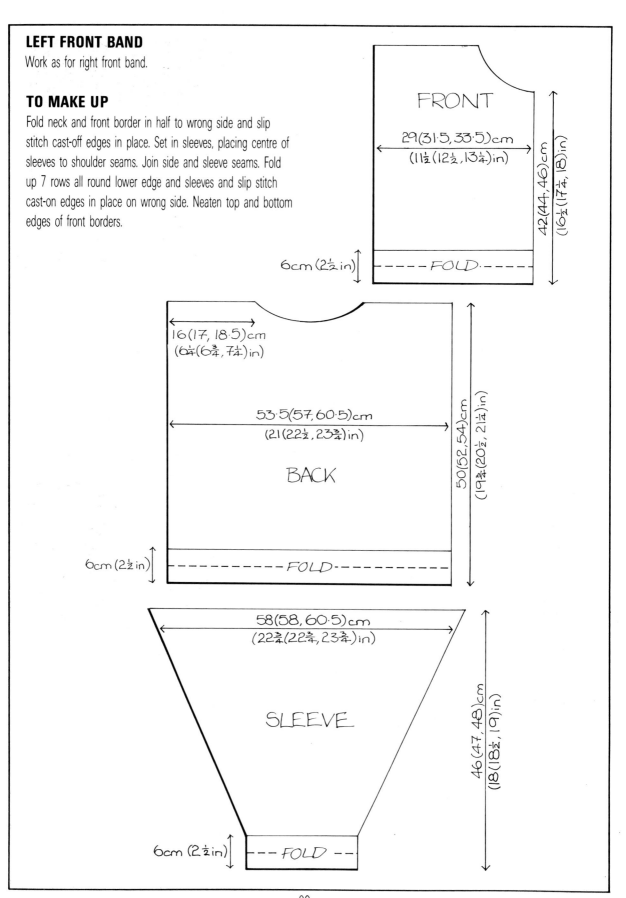

FRONT

29(31·5, 33·5)cm
(11½(12½, 13¾)in)

42(44, 46)cm
(16½(17¼, 18)in)

6cm (2½ in)

FOLD

16(17, 18·5)cm
(6¼(6¾, 7¼)in)

53·5(57, 60·5)cm
(21(22½, 23¾)in)

BACK

50(52, 54)cm
(19¾(20½, 21¼)in)

6cm (2½ in)

FOLD

58(58, 60·5)cm
(22¾(22¾, 23¾)in)

SLEEVE

46(47, 48)cm
(18(18½, 19)in)

6cm (2½ in)

FOLD

VARIATIONS

WORK STRIPES IN
CONTRAST FOR MULTI
COLOURED EFFECT

VARIATIONS

POLO BECOMES CLASSIC CREW NECK BY RIBBING 6CM (2½IN) DOUBLE OVER TO WRONG SIDE SLIP STICH INTO PLACE

ORANGE GRANDEUR

VARIATIONS

CLASSIC SLIPOVER
SHORTENED

WORK LESS STRIPES
FOR BOXY LOOK

LONGER LENGTH
FOR MORE
SOPHISTICATED
LOOK

RED HOT

WORK EXTRA STRIPES
FOR LONGER SKIRT

ALL
STRIPED UP

VARIATIONS

WORK EXTRA STRIPES
FOR LONGER SKIRT

NIFTY NAUTICAL

VARIATIONS

INSTANTLY TRANSFORM THIS DRESS INTO A SWEATER BY WORKING LESS ROWS

PASTEL POWER

VARIATIONS

FOR 'V-NECK', WORK
TO END OF COLLAR
SHAPING – CAST OFF

HOODWINKED.